VAISNAVA SOCIETY
Volume 6

"Remembering TKG & George"

RUPANUGA VEDIC COLLEGE

Edited by His Holiness Danavir Goswami

Layout by Arya-siddhanta Dasa
Cover Design Gaura-hari Dasa and Arya-siddhanta Dasa
Published by Rupanuga Vedic College © 2003
ISBN: 0972837205
Printed and bound in India by Gopsons Papers Ltd.
A-14, Sector 60, Noida 201 301
Special Thanks to Radha Jivan Dasa

RUPANUGA VEDIC COLLEGE

5201 The Paseo
Kansas City, Missouri 64110
Tel: (816) 924-5619
Fax: (816) 924-5640
E-Mail: rvc@rvc.edu
Website: www.rvc.edu

Contents

VAISNAVA SOCIETY
Volume 6

"Remembering TKG & George"

CHAPTER 1: CULTURE

DRIVING FOR KRISHNA

By His Holiness Danavir Goswami

From its early years to present, ISKCON has witnessed droves of devotees leave their bodies while traveling in automobiles. Although devotees don't drink and drive, many male devotee drivers that I know are virtual terrors behind the wheel. With a desire to reduce Vaisnava auto tragedies and hoping to improve our service to Lord Krishna, Srila Prabhupada and our spiritual authorities, we humbly suggest some guidelines for devotee drivers to follow.

Let us begin by understanding that driving an automobile in the service of the Lord (dasyam) is equal to performing any other service in bhakti-yoga such as sravanam, kirtanam, distributing books, offering arati to the deities, managing a temple, etc. Sri Daruka, Sri Hanuman, Sri Garuda and other devotees are famous for rendering the service of transporting the Lord from one place to another.

Srila Prabhupada wanted devotees to drive carefully and he censured careless driving on several occasions. If we ignore his request and the laws governing safe driving, we are spiritually and materially at fault[1]. Due to inattention in performing devotional service, a careless devotee driver may not achieve the highest destination should he be called upon to leave his body. The Katha Upanisad (1.3.14) warns: ksurasya dhara nisita duratyaya durgam pathas tat kavayo vadanti. "The path of spiritual realization is very difficult; it is sharp like a razor's edge. That is the opinion of learned transcendental scholars."[2]

CARELESS DRIVING IS NOT AUTHORIZED[3]

Speeding:[4]

> *Actually, we are seeing, especially in the Western countries, this motorcar civilization, when we run on the motorcar, especially with high speed, it is always we think that any moment danger can take place. (aside:) You remember, you were driving your father's car, eighty miles. So I asked you, "Don't go so fast." (Class given by Srila Prabhupada in Vrndavana, November 10, 1972)*
>
> *Prabhupāda: They are not sober. Adhīra. Therefore they meet with so many accidents. You also. As soon as we're in the car, he wants to drive at a hundred miles speed.*
> *Puṣṭa Kṛṣṇa: I think it was token punishment, but I'm sorry if you were in the car. [Referring to an car accident in Africa which Srila Prabhupada was in the car]*
> *Prabhupāda: (laughs) What is the use? You are not going to serve anyone that we have to go high speed. We can go comfortably.*
> *Hari-śauri: We can make our own pace.*
> *Prabhupāda: Yes. Śyāmasundara also. He was driving seventy-five. And what you are doing? What is that? This country, Portland.*
> *Puṣṭa Kṛṣṇa: Oregon? From Eugene to Oregon.*
> *Prabhupāda: Oregon, yes.*
> *Puṣṭa Kṛṣṇa: I was in the car with you in the back seat.*
> *Prabhupāda: Oh, you were in the car?*
> *Puṣṭa Kṛṣṇa: They all fell asleep. I was chanting. You were sitting, you didn't even go to sleep that night (laughs). Even though it was late at night, it was about eleven, twelve, one o'clock at night, you didn't want to stay at that bhogī yogi house. I remember that. And he drove very, very fast back to Portland. That was a very nice engagement.*
> *Prabhupāda: Hmm. That was Śyāmasundara's father's car. So he's a good driver, (laughter) but very dangerous driver. (Room Conversation — June 18, 1976, Toronto)*

Here Srila Prabhupada is speaking to his disciple Syamasundara dasa about the time five months before when Syamasundara drove Srila Prabhupada in Oregon. I was also onboard that late-model Chevrolet loaned by Syamasundara's father. Certainly Srila Prabhupada knew that Krishna was in control and that Krishna protects His devotees, still he did not approve of fast driving.[5]

For momentary exhilaration, devotee-drivers behave like rebels without a cause putting aside even common sense. Reckless driving is practically suicidal but suicide is not approved for devotees.

Tailgating:

Tailgating is the practice of following another vehicle too closely. This practice is common among passionate materialist drivers and unfortunately is found among large percentages of male devotee drivers. Such behavior cannot be considered Krishna-conscious since it has no valuable purpose and is most foolish.

Late-night driving:

> *It will be a good idea in the future if our devotees take lesson from this unfortunate incident and take precaution not to drive late at night for any reason—no gain can come from such driving at night which will ever compensate for much great losses. Please advise your GBC zonal secretary that in future great precaution must be taken.(Letter from Srila Prabhupada to: Patita Uddharana—Delhi 15 November, 1971)*

Enough said.

Japa-bag driving:

It is nice to chant while driving but it is not safe to keep the hand in the bead bag and try to drive. At any moment the driver may have to swerve quickly and the beanbag can get entangled in the steering wheel. When driving, better to chant on one's fingers.

Eyes on the road:

Sometimes devotee drivers carry on conversations with others in their vehicle while they drive and while doing so they like to look at the person they are speaking with. I have experienced devotee drivers turning around to look at someone in the back seat while speaking with the person.

Drowsy driving:

Devotees don't sleep very much but driving to distant places requires plenty of rest. A devotee should generally expect to sleep at least eight hours if he/she plans to drive more than a hour at a time. Also devotee drivers must have a policy that as soon as it becomes difficult to keep the eyes open he must immediately stop and take some rest.

Sloka memorization:

It is nice to memorize slokas but taping slokas on the speedometer is going too far.

DRIVING FOR KRISHNA RULES

Rule #1: Never go faster than the posted speed limit posted.

Rule #2: Never follow closely behind the vehicle in front.[6]

Rule #3: Drive gently and politely.[7]

Rule #4: Stop driving as soon as the eyelids become difficult to keep open.

Rule #5: On single lane highways, do not dangerously pass slower vehicles.[8] Shanti.

Rule #6: Drivers should be capable[9] and confident drivers with valid driving licenses.[10]

Rule #7: Vehicles must be safe; i.e. brakes, tires, rear view mirrors, horn, etc.

Rule #8: Drivers must follow all traffic signs explicitly.[11]

Rule #9: Drivers should not chant on beads while driving (they may chant on their fingers as did Lord Caitanya[12])

Rule #10: Drivers must wear glasses if needed.

26 QUALITIES OF A DEVOTEE DRIVER

With the readers' permission, we have taken some liberties in applying these terms to driving. Here is the actual translation: "Devotees are always merciful, humble, truthful, equal to all, faultless, magnanimous, mild and clean. They are without material possessions, and they perform welfare work for everyone. They are peaceful, surrendered to Krsna and desireless. They are indifferent to material acquisitions and are fixed in devotional service. They completely control the six bad qualities—lust, anger, greed and so forth. They eat only as much as required, and they are not inebriated. They are respectful, grave, compassionate and without false prestige. They are friendly, poetic, expert and silent."

While driving, I humbly suggest that a devotee or aspiring devotee should put into practice Vaisnava devotional principles such as described by Lord Krishna in the eleventh canto, verses 29-32 of the Srimad Bhagavatam and again mentioned by Sri Caitanya Mahaprabhu in Caitanya Caritamrita, Madhya-lila 22.78-80 as follows:

(1) krpalu—merciful
Example: A Krishna-conscious driver doesn't want to endanger the passengers in his vehicle or those in other vehicles by driving recklessly.

(2) akrta-droha—humble;
Example: A Krishna-conscious driver obeys all the traffic laws.

(3) satya-sara—truthful;
Example: A Krishna-conscious driver practices not driving even slightly over the speed limit, even if there are no police officers nearby, knowing how this will lead to further excesses.

(4) sama—equal;
Example: A Krishna-conscious driver knows that all vehicles have the same type of spirit souls (jivatma) inside and each living being is subject to illusion, to make mistakes, to cheat and to possess imperfect senses. Consequently, he expects them to do something dangerous and thus he drives defensively.

(5) nidosa—faultless;
Example: A Krishna-conscious driver is never the cause of an accident due to his self-indulgent driving.

(6) vadanya—magnanimous;
Example: A Krishna-conscious driver allows a very broad distance between his vehicle and the one in front of his vehicle.

(7) mrdu—mild;
Example: A Krishna-conscious driver tolerates stopping at red lights.

(8) suci—clean;
Example: A Krishna-conscious driver keeps the windshields, mirrors, and windows free from dirt.

(9) akincana—without material possessions;
Example: A Krishna-conscious driver does not use a cell phone while driving.

(10) sarva-upakaraka—working for the welfare of everyone;
Example: A Krishna-conscious driver recognizes that by driving safely his chances of performing more sankirtana are increased.

(11) santa—peaceful;
Example: A Krishna-conscious driver is not in a frantic hurry to arrive some place quickly.

(12) krsna-eka-sarana—exclusively surrendered to Krsna;

Example: A Krishna-conscious driver understands that his body belongs to Krishna and therefore he does not gamble it away in impulsive driving.

(13) akama—desireless;

Example: A Krishna-conscious driver does not have the inclination to be "ahead" of other vehicles.

(14) aniha—indifferent to material acquisitions;

Example: A Krishna-conscious driver does not drive faster than the speed limit even though his speedometer indicates that the vehicle is capable of traveling at higher speeds.

(15) sthira—fixed;

Example: A Krishna-conscious driver always wears his seat belt and makes sure that other passengers do so as well.

(16) vijita-sat-guna—completely controlling the six bad qualities (lust, anger, greed, etc.);

Example: A Krishna-conscious driver does not curse at others, make menacing gestures toward others or in other words lose his temper while driving.

(17) mita-bhuk—eating only as much as required;

Example: A Krishna-conscious driver does not eat while driving.

(18) apramatta—without inebriation;

Example: A Krishna-conscious driver does not try to get some stimulation from fast driving.

(19) mana-da—respectful;

Example: A Krishna-conscious driver allows other vehicles to enter his lane before his vehicle as required.

(20) amani—without false prestige;

Example: A Krishna-conscious driver agrees to move into the right lane (slower lane) allowing faster vehicles to surpass him using the left lane (faster lane).

(21) gambhira—grave;

Example: A Krishna-conscious driver never forgets how dangerous it is to drive a motor vehicle. This material world is a place where danger lurks at every step. Padam padam yad vipadam na tesam.

(22) karuna—compassionate;

Example: A Krishna-conscious driver sets a good example for others to follow both in his driving and his consciousness.

(23) maitra—friendly;

Example: A Krishna-conscious driver is the best friend to all other drivers and pedestrians because he is so careful.

(24) kavi—poetic;

Just drive for Krishna
No speeding and no reading
No daring and no swearing
Just drive for Krishna

(25) daksa—expert;

Example: A Krishna-conscious driver considers driving a vehicle his precious service to the Lord and thus he performs this duty like Daruka.

(26) mauni—silent.

Example: A Krishna-conscious driver does not talk so much that it distracts his driving.

CONCLUSION

We hope that by safe driving, the numbers of devotee-drivers and their passengers who are forced to leave their bodies will be diminished. Nevertheless, if it is our time to depart, we want to be sure that we are performing our duty properly, namely driving carefully for Krishna.

Endnotes:

1. Just like when we are driving car, the law is red light, we have to stop. That is law. Because if you unrestrictedly drive your car, there will be accident. Either you will die or somebody will die. (Srila Prabhupada's Lecture on Śrīmad-Bhāgavatam 1.3.9—Los Angeles, September 15, 1972)
2. One may drive well, or else one may drive whimsically, in which case it is quite possible that he may have an accident and fall into a ditch. In other words, if one takes directions from the experienced spiritual master one can go back home, back to Godhead; otherwise, one may return to the cycle of birth and death. (SB 7.15.41 Purport)
3.Rādhā-vallabha: In New Jersey one time we were driving very fast to try and meet you at the airport, and a police officer pulled us over, and he was very angry. We were driving very fast. And he said...
Prabhupāda: No, you should not drive fast. (devotees laugh) No, no, this is not good.
Rādhā-vallabha: We had to pick you up at the airport, Prabhupāda, and we were late.
Prabhupāda: That's all right, but fast, drive very fast, is risky.
Rādhā-vallabha: So this police officer he pulled us over. He was very angry. He said, "Let us see your license and registration." We gave it to him, and it said International Society for Kṛṣṇa Consciousness on the registration. He said, "Oh, Kṛṣṇa." And he asked us some questions about the philosophy, and he listened very carefully, and then he said, "I cannot give people like you a ticket." [break]
Prabhupāda: ...they are pleased, but don't take undue advantage. Yes. (Morning Walk—June 26, 1975, Los Angeles)
4. Human decision that there is signboard, "Speed Limit 35." If he doesn't care, he is not a human being, he is animal. A human being, he will take care, "Why shall I drive 100?" (Srila Prabhupada discussing on Jean-Paul Sartre)
5. Leave a minimum of one car length for each ten miles per hour or 16 kilometers per hour of speed you are traveling. In other words, if you are traveling at 60 miles per hour or 96 kilometers per hour then you should remain at least six car lengths behind the vehicle in front of you.
6. Nobody is careful. So that is the position. Unless one is careful to his sense that "Why should I drive so fiercely or without any care that others may be injured, my car will be

injured? Why shall I created this trouble? Let me drive the car very conscientiously..." So that is required. (Lecture on Śrīmad-Bhāgavatam 1.8.51—Los Angeles, May 13, 1973)
7. In the Western countries, especially in America, it is very nice to possess a good car, but as soon as one is on the road, there is danger because at any moment an accident may take place and one will be killed. The record actually shows that so many people die in such accidents. (SB 8.2.32 Purport)
8. If you do not know how to drive, then the car will play disaster. Your life will be risky. Your life will be risky. If you simply sit down in a good car without knowing the art of driving, then it will play disaster. You give at once motion, and it will collide with something, and you will be fractured, and whole thing will be dismantled. (Bhagavad-gītā Lecture Excerpts: 2.44-45, 2.58 — New York, March 25, 1966)
9. Expert does not mean that I do not know how to drive motor car, and I will have to imitate somebody, "Oh, I shall become driver." Why? If you do not know driving, why should you attempt driving? Whatever you know, you just try it, that business, and try to satisfy Krsna. If you know driving, that's all right. (Srila Prabhupada speaking: Room Conversation — July 16, 1968, Montreal)
10. Suppose you will drive a motor car. That is a sort of work in the street. There is injunction that "You should drive on the right. You should stop your car when there is red light. You should not proceed an inch." So, so many regulations, even for your driving car, anything... Anything of your life—you want to do—there are directions, proper directions from the authorities. (Bhagavad-gītā 3.13-16 — New York, May 23, 1966)
11 Caitanya Mahaprabhu used to count on His fingers. (Caitanya-caritamrita; Madhya 7.37 Purport)

BEET SUGAR

By His Holiness Danavir Goswami

Recently in Kansas City, the RVC has shifted its purchase of white sugar to beet sugar. It was quite simple. We contacted our local supplier and indicated we wanted exclusively beet sugar. The two major types of refined sugar produced in the United States are cane sugar and beet sugar. Most cane sugar uses a filtering process made from cow bones whereas beet sugar does not.

Beet sugar refineries never use a bone char filter in processing because this type of sugar does not require an extensive decolourising procedure. Beet sugar can be refined with a pressure lead filter and an ion exchange system. Western Sugar Co. uses lime as a filter.

Cane sugar and beet sugar cost, look and taste the same and are nutritionally equivalent as well. The production and sale of each type of sugar are approximately equal.

Some of the larger beet sugar manufacturers are:

Western Sugar Co.—Baynard, Nebraska (308) 586-1511 or Lovell, Wyoming (307) 548-2292
Imperial Sugar Corporation [Holly Sugar is beet sugar] Sugar Land, Texas (281) 491-9181
Michigan Sugar Company—Bay City, Michigan (517) 799-7300

Great Lakes Sugar Company—Freemont, Ohio (419) 332-9931

I also confirmed this information by contacting several sugar manufacturers.

Much information provided above and all of that provided below was acquired from Caroline Pyevich's article "Sugar and other sweeteners: Do they contain animal products." (Vegetarian Journal: excerpts March/April, 1997)

Many cane refineries use bone char. Domino, the largest sugar manufacturer in the U.S., uses bone char in the filtration process. The cane refineries of Savannah Foods, the second largest sugar manufacturer, also use bone char. California and Hawaiian Sugar employs bone char filters in addition to granular carbon and ion exchange filters. All these companies use the bone char in the refining process of brown sugar, powdered sugar (sugar mixed with corn starch) and white sugar.

Almost all cane sugar refineries require the use of a specific filter to decolourise the sugar and absorb inorganic material from it. This whitening process occurs towards the end of the sugar refining procedure. The filter may be either bone char, granulated carbon, or an ion exchange system. The granular carbon has a wood or coal base, and the ion exchange does not require the use of any animal products.

Bones from cows are the only type used to make bone char. According to the Sugar Association and several large sugar producers, all of the cows have died of natural causes and do not come from the U.S. meat industry. Bone char cannot be produced or bought in the United States. Bone char is derived from the bones of cattle from Afghanistan, Argentina, India and Pakistan. The sun-bleached bones are bought by Scottish, Brazilian, and Egyptian marketers, who sell them to the U.S. sugar industry after the bones are first used by the gelatin industry.

Bone is heated to an extremely high temperature, which results in a physical change in the bones composition. The bone becomes pure carbon before it is used in a refinery. Refined sugar does not contain any bone particles and is therefore kosher certified. The bone char simply removes impurities from the sugar, but does not become a part of the sugar.

Some cane refineries do not use bone char. Refined Sugar, producers of Jack Frost Sugar, claim to use a granular carbon instead of bone char for economic reasons. Florida Crystal sugar is a cane sugar which has not passed through the bone. Although Florida Crystals sugar has a straw colour, the impurities have been removed.

DIVINITY DEGREES

LETTER TO RVC DIRECTOR

E-mail: Leroy.Wade@mocbhe.gov Web Site: www.cbhe.state.mo.us
Telephone: 573-751-2361 Fax: 573-751-6635

Dear Dr. Holtzman: June 17, 2002

This is in response to your request for information concerning the status of Rupanuga Vedic College (RVC) under Missouri statutes. As the person responsible for the administration of the Department of Higher Education's postsecondary school oversight program, I am happy to provide you with the following information.

Based on the information contained in the department files, RVC continues to be an institution that is exempt from the requirements for certification to operate as described in sections 173.600 through 173.618, RSMo. Although our most recent update of material was provided in October of 2000, your assurance that material continues to be applicable would seem to reinforce continued exemption. Although we have plans to initiate a routine verification process with exempt schools, those plans are currently on hold.

If you wish to confirm your status in writing, please send us a current copy of the current school catalog along with a request for verification.

It is our hope that the relationship between the school and the Department of Higher Education is one of cooperation. It is our goal to serve as a clearinghouse for information about postsecondary education in the state. That goal is best served through clear communication and collaboration, even when a school is not subject to the operational requirements established by the department.

As an exempt institution, the religiously designated degrees conferred by RVC are legal in the state. Any conclusion concerning their legitimacy or validity (beyond the strict legal sense) is beyond the scope of the department's authority. Such determinations are usually the province of the higher education community. In general, accreditation by a recognized accrediting commission will convey more acceptance within that community that the determination of legality can provide.

I hope this information is helpful. If you have questions or need any additional information, please do not hesitate to contact us.

Leroy Wade
Director, Proprietary School Certification
Missouri Coordinating Board for Higher Education
3515 Amazonas Drive
Jefferson City, MO 65109

RVC: OFFERING SPIRITUAL DEGREES

By Dr. S. Arnold

I'm expressing my opinion with regards to some letters that appeared on Chakra concerning the worthlessness of degrees offered by RVC [Rupanuga Vedic College]. I believe that may be true on a material level because RVC is apparently not a "materially accredited" university. I believe obtaining a degree at this university is not meant for temporary material pursuits, pride, worldly recognition, and personal sense gratification or to pursue temporary material jobs. However, my limited understanding of this matter is that the knowledge gained at this institution and the degrees offered are everlasting and take one beyond the temporary illusion of material nature.

In conclusion, these degrees may appear worthless in this material world, unrecognized by worldly universities that use imperfect senses to do their accreditation, but clearly this is pure knowledge that unfortunately few realized souls will experience, that will ultimately take them back to the spiritual world. I believe the RVC is well recognized and accredited in the "real eternal spiritual world."

I believe these students and devotees will be getting real knowledge and real degrees that will result in their liberation and return back to the permanent, spiritual world, free of the material illusion that the majority of us find ourselves in.

All glories to Srila Prabhupada.

Your fallen soul, your servant

Dr. S. Arnold

Newfoundland, Canada

SRILA PRABHUPADA ON DIVINE EDUCATION

Tamāla Kṛṣṇa: It seems like for the first few years you were... Our movement was very much engaged in establishing our centers, but now it seems that we can concentrate on actually pushing forward the knowledge we have to give.

Prabhupāda: Centers were meant for that purpose, for giving knowledge, not for show, a church, a show. What is knowledge?

Tamāla Kṛṣṇa: Now we have our centers established.

Prabhupāda: Yes.

Tamāla Kṛṣṇa: So we can concentrate on...

Prabhupāda: Giving knowledge.

(Letter from Yugoslavia—"Books!" — June 30, 1977, Vṛndāvana)

Therefore, these meetings which we hold every day, they are meant for advancing in spiritual life. Here, there is no program how to become very rich, how to possess more motorcars, how to have more bank balance, how to have nice dress. These are material things. Or ignorance: how to sleep thirty-four hours a day, although we have got twenty-four hours only. (Lecture: Bhagavad-gītā 2.16 — London, August 22, 1973)

And from the very beginning, if they begin education with Bhagavad-gītā and then comes to Śrīmad-Bhāgavatam and reads the whole literature, then they will be more than M.A., Ph.D. More than. The knowledge will be so advanced. (Śrīmad-Bhāgavatam 1.16.22 — Los Angeles, July 12, 1974)

SRILA PRABHUPADA ON SECULAR EDUCATION

There is no need to learn Bengali. I do not encourage learning any new skills. Whatever material abilities one has when he comes to Krsna consciousness, let him learn to engage these in Krsna's service: that is sufficient. There is no need of learning new skills now. That will simply be a waste of time. (Letter to: Dasanudasa — Hrsikesa 13 May, 1977)

Regarding your proposal to become a doctor, because your mother wants to prosecute your education, I think if you can learn Krishna Consciousness perfectly, by reading our different literatures, and books, you will be a better doctor than the ordinary physician. The ordinary physician may cure the disease of the body, but if you become advanced in Krishna Consciousness, you will be able to cure the disease of the soul for many many persons. And that is more important than a doctor or medical practitioner for curing the disease of this body. However we may be expert for keeping this body fit, it is sure and certain that this will end. But if you can protect the soul from being fallen a victim of this material existence that is a greater service. In some of the Vedic literatures, it is said that Atmanan Sarvato Rakshet, that means one should give first protection to the soul. Then he should take care of his particular type of faith, then he should take care of the material things, namely this body, and anything in relation with this body, or wealth. Please try to read all our books very carefully, and whenever there is any doubt, you ask me, and be expert preacher. That will make you a great doctor for protecting the human society from being fallen a victim to maya. (Letter to: Tosana Krsna — Seattle 7 October, 1968)

Mother: Well, I didn't mean yours in particular. I'm talking now of all of you. I'm not talking of you particularly. I'm talking of all of you. All your children, the married devotees...?

Prabhupāda: Yes, our children, we have got our own school. All these boys, they have got their children. They are gṛhasthas, householders. So we have got our nice school at Dallas, very big school.

Mother: But you have got a school, a Kṛṣṇa school?

Prabhupāda: Yes, oh, yes.

Mother: And now, how...? Do they go through college?

Prabhupāda: They are now little children. But we don't wish to send them to college. We have got sufficient books.

Mother: So you'll cut off their education like that?

Prabhupāda: What is this nonsense education?

Revatīnandana: No, no.

Mother: Now, do you think that's not cruel to them?

Prabhupāda: We don't care for this...

Revatīnandana: We cut off your education, and we take education from the Vedas and from our spiritual master. We learn how to read, how to write, how to handle numbers sufficiently, and whatever we need practically for our work. And we learn the science of God from our spiritual master. And we find that sufficient for us. We haven't got to spend extra time and many extra years irrelevant subjects that are never going to relate to our practical life or to our God conscious life.

Jesuit Priest: But you're depending on other people, then, to do the other side of your life for you.

Prabhupāda: We are not depending on anyone.

Jesuit Priest: Well, what happens when suddenly one of you gets, very ill tomorrow morning?

Prabhupāda: Eh? What is that?

Jesuit Priest: What happens if somebody gets very ill tomorrow morning?

Prabhupāda: So we give them medicine.

Mother: You call the doctor.

Jesuit Priest: No, you call the doctor, don't you?

Prabhupāda: So we pay for that.

Jesuit Priest: I know, but you call him, don't you? You want him to be, you want the doctor in existence.

Prabhupāda: So does it mean to say that because we require necessary, we have to take education of medical man?

Mother: But you don't train people to be medical men.

Prabhupāda: No, first of all, if we can get it easily...

Mother: Yes.

Prabhupāda: Our training is... First of all, try to understand. We... Just like you have got four divisions in the body for maintaining the body. So the head division, the arm division, the belly division, and the leg division. The leg is doing its own work, walking. The hand is doing its own work. And the belly's doing its own work. And the brain is doing own work. It does not mean that when the brain is work, it does not require the help of the leg. But a brain does not require to learn the business of the leg. This is the idea. The brain requires the help of the leg. But does not mean that brain has to learn how to walk also.

Mother: Well, I'm a nurse, and so that is why I would like...

Prabhupāda: So there must be division of work. So you take from... When there is necessity of brain work, you take help from him. And when there is need of the walking, take leg, help from the leg. It is a cooperation. Not that everyone has to learn everything.

Mother: Yes. Well, as I say...

Prabhupāda: It does not...

Mother: I myself did a training. I became a nurse.

Prabhupāda: You are asking us "Why you are not taking medical education?" Why we shall take?

Mother: Because if everybody...

Prabhupāda: No, there is no necessity. If the... If I can pay, I can get the help of a medical man, why should I waste my time in that way? Let me...

Mother: You think? Ah, but you should be self-supporting. You should be...

Prabhupāda: Let me engage my time for understanding God. (Garden Conversation with Mahādeva's Mother and Jesuit Priest — July 25, 1973, London)

Prabhupāda: The Marwaris in India, they don't educate their son. Just like Birla. They say, "We can purchase these rascals, why we should waste our time. (laughter) So-called technicians, so-called expert computer, these are... We can purchase, why we shall waste our time."

Haṁsadūta: It's the same thing I learned in Germany. First I wanted to get my own press and I studied the situation very carefully and I saw it was ridiculous for us to do that, it's so much hard work. It's much easier to collect the money in the street by giving the magazine and then paying someone. They work very hard and do it. Everything is like that. They have so many people that can do everything. The one thing that people can't do is distribute Kṛṣṇa consciousness and for that Kṛṣṇa's giving so much money.

Prabhupāda: Yes, therefore tasyaiva hetoḥ prayateta kovidaḥ. That verse.

Only for this purpose one should endeavor.

Haṁsadūta: Yes. Kṛṣṇa (indistinct) paying for that.

Prabhupāda: You cannot purchase Kṛṣṇa consciousness—you can have money—that you have to cultivate.

Revatīnandana: Yeah, when Mr. Birla is getting old then he has to come to us, if he has any sense.

Prabhupāda: No they say, they simply give primary education (indistinct) they can read, that's all. And (indistinct). They don't send because everyone knows that sending boys to the school means spoil them. That's all. I have seen intelligent boys, they go to school and he is spoiled. Yes, spoiled. He learns how to smoke, how to have sex, how to talk nonsense, how to use knife, how to fight, these things. At least at the present moment. Yes. Simply slaughterhouse, this so-called school is called slaughterhouse. Yes, slaughterhouse.

Revatīnandana: It was when I went to school—I was a nice little boy—in school I failed out, only (indistinct).

Prabhupāda: Yes, you must take as intelligent. That so..., time was wasted. Our, this gurukula should be taken care of very nicely. So nice preachers may come out. Brāhmaṇa, nice brāhmaṇa.

tasyaiva hetoḥ prayateta kovido
na labhyate yad bhramatām upary adhaḥ
tal labhyate duḥkhavad anyataḥ sukhaṁ
kālena sarvatra gabhīra-raṁhasā

(Room Conversation — July 9, 1973, London)

Nobody is being educated to become good. So what is the use of these rascal universities? If they are producing greedy and lusty people, then what is the use of education? Vidyā dadāti namratā. Education means everyone should be gentleman. That is education. And if you produce lusty and greedy people there is no... This is animal education. The animals are lusty and greedy. (Conversation with Journalists — August 18, 1971, London)

Regarding organization of the artists, there is no need of wasting time for learning the art from study of texts. We should always remember that our time is very short. I think our artists should be satisfied with whatever they have learned already, that is sufficient. They should be simply be engaged in painting pictures always, and that will teach them the art sufficiently.

In the beginning I was seriouslv corresponding with Indian friends to get some good mrdanga players, but when I found it too difficult to get a man from India some of my students were given the rudimentary lessons in playing and simply by practice they are putting on Sankirtana Party everywhere. My Guru Maharaja used to say that in a foreign land where you cannot speak the language with the natives very nicely, what do you do when there is a fire in your house just to get their help? In such emergency one has to express himself somehow or other to his foreign friends and get their help to extinguish the fire. But if he wants to learn the language first and then talk with the foreign friends to get help, then everything in the meantime would be finished. Similarly if we have to learn and then paint, it will be a long-term affair. But immediately we want so many pictures for all of our books, so all the artists may always be engaged in painting works and that painting itself will gradually teach them how to make things nice. (Letter to: Satsvarupa — Los Angeles 21 April, 1970)

Hayagriva: He also felt that materialistic progress is a possible hindrance.

Prabhupada: Yes. That is very good idea. That is confirmed by Bhaktivinoda Thakura. Jada-vidya jato mayara vaibhava tomara bhajane badha. Material progress means expansion of the external energy, maya, illusion. So we are already in illusion, and therefore we practically see the so-called scientists, so-called philosophers, because they are materially advanced, they cannot understand even what is God and what is our relationship. So this is hindrance, the so-called advancement of material science, of material knowledge, is undoubtedly hindrance. Tomara bhajane badha. (Srila Prabhupada on Carl Gustav Jung)

DIVINITY DEGREES AMIDST TODAY'S LEADERS

Jackson, Jesse L., Jr. (1965-), Democratic member of the House of Representatives from Illinois (1995-). Jackson was born in Greenville, South Carolina, the son of American clergyman and civil rights leader Jesse Jackson. He graduated from North Carolina Agricultural and Technical State University with a bachelor's degree in 1987. He earned a graduate divinity degree from Chicago Theological Seminary in 1990 and a law degree from the University of Illinois in 1993. [14]

Strickland, Ted (1941-), Democratic member of the United States House of Representatives from Ohio (1997-). Strickland was born in Lucasville, Ohio. He received a bachelor's degree in history in 1963 from Asbury College in Wilmore, Kentucky. He earned a master of divinity degree from Asbury Theological Seminary in 1967, and a Ph.D. in counseling psychology from the University of Kentucky in Lexington in 1980.[15]

CHAPTER 2: DEVOTEES

GEORGE PLANS TO DIE IN A HOLY INDIAN VILLAGE WHERE HARE KRISHNAS SAY HE'LL GO TO HEAVEN

Cancer-Stricken Beatle Prepares To Meet His Sweet Lord

PROPPED up in a wheelchair, his gaunt body ravaged by cancer, George Harrison is close to death - but not afraid.

The former Beatle has told friends he hasn't got long to live after being diagnosed with a brain tumour - the third time he's been hit by cancer. But he is calm about his final days, thanks to his unshakable Hare Krishna faith. George has even adopted the life of a Krishna holy man to try to ensure he goes to heaven.

Harrison's biographer, Geoffrey Guiliano, says: "Nine months ago, he decided not to drink or smoke. He wants to get as close as possible to the devotee lifestyle. He's also given up meat, eggs and fish.

"He has even made plans to travel to India so he can die in a holy village and - according to Krishna doctrine - go straight to heaven."

Ex-Beatles producer and old friend George Martin revealed at the weekend: "He knows he is going to die soon and accepts that. George is philosophical. He does realise that everybody has got to die sometime.

"He has been near death many times and he has been rescued many times as well. He is taking it easy and hoping that the thing will go away. He has an indomitable spirit."

George, who had been treated at a private Swiss clinic, flew to his Hawaiian hideaway home last week after two months of aggressive radiotherapy treatment. His doctor says he is still seriously ill.

Weak and tired, George spends most of the day in bed taking instruction from Hare Krishna mentors, visiting the ocean shore and chanting mantras for at least two hours a day.

An on-off devotee of the Hare Krishna movement for more than 30 years, George, 58, takes great comfort from his belief in the next life, describing this world as "like a raindrop on a lotus leaf".

As he says: "There is no such thing as death, only in the physical sense." When doctors informed George in March that the cancer he'd fought twice had spread to his brain, he told his family he didn't want more treatment. He decided to concentrate on preparing for death, using what time he had left giving devotion to Krishna. Wife Olivia finally persuaded him to undergo treatment but no more is planned.

Relaxing at his home in Maui, surrounded by spiritual mentors, George is finally finding contentment. At his side for much of the time is his Hare Krishna tutor, Shyamasundara Dasa. He has been offering George spiritual coaching since last summer, spending much of the day chanting and meditating.

Shyamasundara says: "George has achieved a much higher level of self-realisation than I could ever hope to imagine. He's peaceful and serene to a degree that is very rare at such a young age." According to Krishna custom, George will spend his final days surrounded by his "god brothers" - other devotees. As they chant the Hare Krishna mantra at his bedside and drop water drawn from India's holy rivers in to his mouth, George will clutch a Shaligram, a sacred black stone, in each hand.

The musician has already spoken to devotees at the Krishna Balarama Temple in India, asking them to be ready to administer the last rites if he decides to be airlifted there at the last minute.

Biographer Guilliano says: "For a Hare Krishna, the meeting with God at the moment of death is the most important.

"At the moment, George isn't so ill that he's unaware of what's going on. But obviously, because he has a brain tumour, that could be a concern in the future. "He may end up in a coma - you just don't know - so he is making plans to be taken to India if he wants because if he dies in a certain village, that will absolutely guarantee he will get into heaven."

When George passes away, devotees will put sacred tulsi leaves under his tongue then wash and dress his body in traditional Indian cotton robes. Garlands of flowers will be placed around his neck before his body is cremated to the sound of ancient Vedic hymns. The moving ceremony will be the end of his life's winding spiritual journey, taking George from Liverpool to India, via swinging London and his mansion in genteel Henley.

Growing up in a two-up, two-down terrace in Wavertree, his childhood couldn't have been more removed from the Eastern devotee lifestyle he adopted as an adult. BAPTISED a Catholic, the family weren't overtly religious but George was sure there was a God. As a boy, he felt a divine presence but wasn't sure what it was.

He said later: "This feeling would begin to vibrate right through me and started getting bigger and bigger and faster and faster. "Before I knew what was happening, it was going so fast it was mind-boggling and I'd come out of it really scared." In 1966, he met sitar player Ravi Shankar and things changed forever. Through Ravi, George developed a fascination with Indian culture and spirituality that shaped his life.

He said: "Down through the ages, there has always been a spiritual path - it has been passed on and it always will be. It just happens that India was where the seed was planted." By 1967, George and then wife Patti started to meditate regularly and take an active interest in all things spiritual - spending time with Hindu yogi, Maharishi Mahesh that summer.

In 1969, he was introduced to the Hare Krishna movement when Shyamasundara Dasa turned up at the Beatles' Apple studio. George was enthralled by his new faith and helped the movement set up its London base. He said at the time: "I feel at home with Krishna. I think that there's something that has been there from a previous birth. So it was like a door opening to me at the time, but it was also like a jigsaw puzzle." Apple even released a record of the Krishna group's mantra and the repetitive singing has become a major part of his life.

When an intruder attacked George at his Berkshire mansion two years ago, his first instinct was to shout "Hare Krishna, Hare Krishna" at him. And on one turbulent plane journey, he calmed his nerves with chanting.

George said: "I once chanted the mantra all the way from France to Portugal. I drove for about 23 hours and chanted all the way. It gets you feeling a bit invincible." Sadly, as George now knows only too well, no one is invincible, but with his Hare Krishna faith to guide him, he's feeling strong enough to face the dark days ahead.

George Harrison wrote this introduction to Srila Prabhupada's book, Krsna, The Supreme Personality of Godhead, after donating the money to print it. He is also well known for purchasing Bhaktivedanta Manor, ISKCON's European Headquarters, for Srila Prabhupada and his disciples.

Bhaktivedanta Manor, just north of London, UK, was purchased by George Harrison for ISKCON. [From The Mirror (U.K.) Online]

George Harrison "Battling cancer again"

By Ralph Gowling

09 July, 2001 03:47 GMT

LONDON (Reuters) - Former Beatle George Harrison is reported to have received treatment at a Swiss cancer clinic — his third battle in the past few years against the disease.

Just over 18 months ago, the 58-year-old guitarist and singer survived a life-and-death struggle of a different kind, when a knife-wielding intruder stabbed him in the chest at his home near London.

The Swiss newspaper Sonntagszeitung reported on Sunday that Harrison had been treated for a brain tumour in a cancer hospital in Bellinzona in southern Switzerland. Cancer specialist Franco Cavalli did not deny he was treating Harrison at the San Giovanni hospital but declined to give details, the paper said. According to Sonntagszeitung, Harrison was in Bellinzona in the Italian-speaking south of Switzerland during May and June for radiotherapy. Harrison had rented a house in Luino in Italy, a 40-minute drive from Bellinzona, during the cobalt radiation treatment. Sonntagszeitung said it was not clear whether Harrison was still being treated in Bellinzona or had returned to his house in Hawaii.

British papers carried similar reports on Monday. "(Harrison) was here in May and June...But he is not a patient any more," the Mirror quoted a San Giovanni hospital spokesman as saying. No one at Harrison's record company in London was immediately available for comment on the report. Earlier this year Harrison had a cancer-like sore removed from his lungs at the Mayo Clinic in the United States.

THROAT CANCER SCARE

Harrison overcame throat cancer in 1998, which he blamed on smoking. He was given the all-clear after radiation therapy. "I gave up cigarettes many years ago but had started again for a while and stopped in 1997," he said at the time. "Luckily for me, they found that this nodule was more of a warning than anything else." The former Beatle was almost killed in the attack at his home near London in late 1999. Only the actions of his wife Olivia, who struck the knife-wielding attacker over the head with a poker and table lamp, saved him.

Harrison was known as the "quiet Beatle" when he was the lead guitarist for the band during their heyday in the 1960s. "I guess if you've got to be in a rock group it might as well be the Beatles," he once quipped. Harrison was rated as a major musician in his own right only after the break-up of the "Fab Four". The main claim to fame of the Beatles' youngest member during their reign as the kings of pop music was his devotion to oriental mysticism. He persuaded the other Beatles to travel to India to sit at the feet of the Maharishi Mahesh Yogi. He learned to play the sitar, and incorporated the instrument into a number of their songs.

The reserved Liverpudlian lived for many years in the shadow of John Lennon and Paul McCartney, and was liberated by the band's break-up in 1970 — as one associate said, it was "like recovering from a six-year dose of constipation". He soon released a treble album "All Things Must Pass" which proved his worth as both a guitarist and song-writer, and enjoyed a worldwide smash hit with "My Sweet Lord". In the 1980s he produced films through his own company, HandMade Films, and joined Bob Dylan, Roy Orbison and Tom Petty to found the popular Travelling Wilburys in the 1990s.

A STORY ABOUT GEORGE AND SRILA PRABHUPAD

by Nanda Kumar Das

Hare Krishna Prabhus,

Please accept my humble obeisances. All glories to Srila Prabhupad. All glories to Bhakta George Harrison, who is very dear to His Divine Grace.

I would like to share a story about their connection on one occasion in London. I was traveling with Srila Prabhupad, as well as Syamasundar Das and Pradyumna Das, in 1972 (I have a poor memory for dates. I believe this was the year). Syamasundar was instrumental in connecting George with Srila Prabhupad and our movement and had a lot of association with him. They were close friends. I was in the secretary's office, which was more like a large closet off of Prabhupad's quarters, typing letters, when a head popped in the door, and in a very British accent, someone said, "Hello, is Syamasundar here?"

I looked over and said that he was out and would be back later. I went back to my typing and then did a double take, as it was George. I got up and went over to him and said that I would tell Prabhupad that he was here.

He said, very humbly, "No, no, I don't want to bother him."

I assured him that it would not be a bother, and I went into Prabhupad's room to tell him that he was there. Prabhupad immediately said, "Oh! Have him come in." I went back out and told George that he wanted to see him. He was removing his socks and looked over at me and said, "I get so nervous when I am around His Divine Grace."

I told him that I felt the same way. He had just shaved his beard and cut his hair back to a Beatle's style, and he said, "I just got my hair cut to see

Prabhupad." He was so humble and unassuming. It was like being around a great devotee. It was being around a great devotee. He went into the room and closed the door. I could not stay outside, I had to go in and see the exchange. I opened the door, and George was doing full dandavats and offering both prayers to Prabhupad, with perfect pronunciation. Prabhupad had an ear-to-ear smile. George got up and sat back by the door.

Prabhupad said "Come in, come in" and George edged forward towards Prabhupad's desk, very shy and respectful. Prabhupad said "No, here, here" and patted the asana he was sitting on. George came around his desk to the edge of his asana, and Prabhupad reached out and pulled him into his chest, hugging him, laughing, messing up his hair, and saying, "It is so good to see you. How is Patty?"

They had a wonderful conversation, where at one point George asked him if he should move into the temple and shave his head. I believe he would have if Prabhupad had said yes. But Prabhupad said emphatically "No! You have a great gift for the world in your music. Just continue your music and Krishna will be greatly pleased and He will bless you." Then he said "I will give you some ideas for your songs" and he got out Srila Bhaktivinode's Songbook and went over a number of the songs, reciting the translations for George.

It was soon after this that he wrote "My Sweet Lord." George came daily for a week, along with Ravi Shankar, to have Prabhupad's darsan in the afternoon. Ravi Shankar is a Bengali, so he and Prabhupad talked and laughed together as Bengalis. Of course, Srila Prabhupad's remnants were always a transcendental treasure for all the devotees, and I was blessed to be able to distribute them after His meals. During this week, when I would take the plates away, many of the temple matajis would crowd around, asking "Could I have some of George's remnants, please?"

I have remembered this story so many times over the years, with joy and great respect for Bhakta George. He is truly a humble devotee and a great man. I am currently living on Maui, where George had a home, and the stories from the local people are all good. He spread goodness wherever he went. I am greatly honored to have met him on that occasion, and I send him my love. There is no doubt in my mind about where he is now. I hope to see him again.

Offered to the Vaishnavas with love and respect.

Your servant,

Nanda Kumar Das [narasimha1212@hotmail.com]

SYAMASUNDARA DASA SPEAKS ABOUT GEORGE AND HARE KRISHNA

At that time George came to the Haight Ashbury. I don't know if you've seen photos of him walking around with his heart-shaped glasses. He saw the people chanting Hare Krsna in the streets and he'd kinda begun to get the buzz of Hare Krsna, '67 I think. Yeah. Oh and another thing he had gotten a hold of a record, an early recording made, a 33 and 1/3 album by Prabhupada and some of his disciples, on a label called the "Happening Label" in New York called the "Hare Krsna Mantra." They just sang the whole side of an album of "Hare Krsna Hare Krsna Krsna Krsna Hare Hare" in a chanting form with music. He had gotten a hold of a copy of that somewhere. He'd loved it! He'd been listening to it already for months and he gave copies to John, Paul and everybody. I mean Ringo. They all loved it. So he'd already heard about Hare Krishna, but he'd never met any of the Krishnas or anything. And then in fact he told me on his way home that he was flying back from San Francisco down to LA in a light aircraft. He was staying in LA at the time. A big wind came and it started to crash. The plane started dropping, losing altitude rapidly and started going on its side and he started chanting "Hare Krsna!" at the top of his lungs because they were upside-down in the plane. And as soon as he started chanting the plane righted itself, winds calmed and he landed safely. So he thought from that time that there was something to this chanting.

LONDON

Then, in '68 our spiritual master asked us to go to London. Actually it was our idea. The scene, the center of activity, was sort of shifting from San Francisco to London. Things were happening in London then. There was the Carnaby Street fashions and the Beatles and the Rolling Stones. Everything was shifting to London about '68. So Prabhupada had always wanted to have a center in London because he was an Indian and the British Empire. He always thought about London as this vast Wizard of Oz type city in the sky that should have a Krsna Temple. So we took off. We went to London.

And by December we had shifted to an unheated warehouse in Betterton Street which was in Covin Garden an old fruit and vegetable market. It was all warehouses and some wealthy philanthropist gave us to use this old vegetable warehouse. So we were living in there without any heat. Right in the center of London though. And one day I got a call from the Airport from Rock Skully. And he had just flown in with Ken Keezy and some of the Grateful Dead members and Sonny Barger. I think it was Mickey...Mickey Heart. Was that his name? Yeah. Somebody like that. That's not clear in mind because that person didn't stay with us, but Rock did and Ken Keezy and

Sonny Barger and some other major Hells Angels. And they had brought their choppers on the on the plane as cargo and they were gonna take London by storm. They were gonna go meet the Beatles and start a chapter of Hells Angles and turn London into San Francisco. This was their plan.

So Rock called me up from the airport and I got out and picked them up. I had a pick-up truck. So we could put their motorcycles in the back of the pick-up, and I took them all to our warehouse and they came and stayed with us, but not very long. They didn't like the idea of taking their boots off at the door (laughter) and sleeping on the floor in the sleeping bag, but they did stay with us a couple of days. And then about a week later I got a call from Rock and he says "Yeah. Were going out to meet the Beatles today. We've got an invitation to go up" So, I said "Well, geez do you mind if we tag along?" He said, "No. Come on." So we went up. 3 Sally Road was their address in those days and they had a huge reception room upstairs. So I went up there and it was filled with people. Maybe 100 people. All famous kind of people and Ken Keezy and the Hells Angels and all these people waiting around to see the Beatles. The Beatles were apparently in a conference in another room. So they were going to come in and everyone was going to meet them.

Well, hours and hours people waited and I sat over in a far corner at the very farthest point from this door where they were. And then suddenly, at one point the door opened up and George stuck his head out the door, looked around the room, put it back. Just dashed back. And then he looked out again and He saw me over there and he just walked right through all those people. Came over to me and sat down and he said... His first words were, "Where have you been? I've been waiting to meet you."

And then he came over to our little center. We heard this little narrow street in the middle of the day and this roaring muffler and it was George in his Porsche pulling up onto the curb, dashing out in a big black fluffy coat. And he came up and had prasadam with us. Prasadam means food offered to Krsna.

HARE KRISHNA RECORD

It [the Hare Krishna record] was released and it became a big smash hit in England and then all over Europe. All over the world basically except America. They wouldn't release it in America. There was some politics involved with, I think religious movements or something. Catholics maybe didn't want it. Who knows? It never got played, never got released in America.

Big Hit in England. We were on top of the pops. We made a video—one of the first rock videos was done with us. Were walking down the street. Oxford Street. Down the streets of London chanting "Hare Krsna" cuz they couldn't just sit us in a room and have us... it just wasn't flamboyant enough. They wanted a whole scene and color. Anyway and Yugoslavia— number one. Japan— number one. It just went all around the world. Australia. Even some of the countries in Africa bought two or three hundred copies. We'd get the print-outs everyday from Apple how many sold in each country. It was really interesting.

A TALK WITH THE FAB FOUR

I probably should back track a little bit. At one point when they were filming the "Let it Be." It was a kind of a film and record same time at Turkanham Studios. George asked me to come out one day. He says, "I want you to speak to the boys." So I came out there and I didn't have a pass to get in or anything, but I was standing by the gate with hundreds of other fans and groupies wondering what to do. And then John and Yoko pulled up in a big white Rolls and I just kinda crouched down beside her window. She gave me a wink out the window and I walked through the gate like this, crouched down and then stood up when I got in and all these people were walking around in costumes. The guy who plays Dracula that...What was his name? Christopher?...(Oh. Christopher Lee?) Yeah. Well, that guy who always played Dracula, he walked by in costume and so nobody noticed me. I'm in a costume. (Laughter). So I walked on the set, sat down in a corner, chanted while I watched these guys kinda... They were arguing and stuff. You know. Starting to come unraveled a little bit. Then at lunch time, around one o'clock perhaps, They broke and George says come on with us. We went up into a room. A room where they were having lunch, but there were only the four Beatles and myself. Not even Yoko. And they all sat each in one corner and I sat in the middle, kind of at the end of the room. I think it was John said, "Ok. Tell us what it's all about then." (Laughter)

So, I had an hour to preach Krsna Consciousness and I started out explaining that Krsna is just another name for God. That there are so many names for God, but Krsna is the name for God as a person in his most opulent and supreme form, as the most beautiful and all attractive personality. And He advented, He was actually on this earth about 5000 years ago in India. And everything about Him is documented. It's not like the Bible or one of those scriptures that doesn't tell you very much about God. Everything Krsna did from the time he was a baby is written about. All those things he did. His adventures and his pastimes that went on for decades in India 5000 years ago. Plus the only scripture that exists on this planet written by God, spoken by God is called the Bhagavad-gita. Song of God. And that is the key text that we use because Krsna explains there who He is and what all this is about in a very short form. A very succinct form that anyone can understand.

So anyway, I explained to them about who Krsna is and about Bhagavad-gita. How it explains that this material world is only a fleeting expansion of Krsna's energy that the spirit souls get trapped in due to misdeeds perhaps or some kind of a desire to be here and enjoy their material senses. But that the larger existence, that exists beyond all this, where you can go and can leave this material world and actually enter that realm also through certain practices. And the practices lead you ultimately to pure love of God. If you can enter that state of consciousness called God consciousness which is nothing but pure unalloyed love for God. Then you've reached the highest state of human development. And being God conscious doesn't mean you surrender giving up your senses or anything like that. We all have five senses. You know, our tongue, our noses, our ears, our touch and our eyes. And it doesn't mean you give up those things that you use now to enjoy the material things. Feeding things. Passing things. You use them spiritually. You surrender those to seeing Krsna in things. You surrender to hearing Krsna in things. You're touching Krsna in things. In other words just transform your senses. Don't give them up. Transform them. That's all. And then you begin to take part in the transcendental or eternal ecstasy that exists beyond this material realm. And it works. It really works. The proof is in the pudding, you know. By practicing it you begin to see, "Oh yeah, this really works!" And this is from a person who is the most skeptical of all [referring to himself]. You know, a philosopher and a drug addict. And everyone who knows about those things knows that those are the ultimate extremes of trying to find out the truth. I mean, if I'm under some drug, in some drug induced state, I'm under the illusion that I'm in pure ecstasy or pure fantasy, pleasure. Oh this feels great! But there's nothing comparable to the spiritual world. It's so much higher, the pleasure that you get. Well, anyway I explained all these things to these four boys and they were curious. They asked questions, but George was really the only one that really drank it in like a sponge.

7 BURY PLACE

Meanwhile, we had found a building in downtown London that somehow had got overlooked in some kind of litigation or something and was available to us for—What did we pay for that thing? 30 pounds per week or something? Some small amount of money. We got a seven story building in downtown London, just off Oxford Street. Just Krsna gave it to us. So, we began building that up to get it ready for Prabhupada to come over from San Francisco. And George was very helpful on that. He signed a guarantorship that we would pay the rent if we had ever failed, that Apple would pay it. So that gave us the lease. Then he contributed the marble. A very expensive slab of marble for the altar piece and in small ways he helped all the time. Always helping.

While we were building the temple. Well, that place was torn up. The building was torn up. So I told George that we just don't have any place to hang out. We're kinda' hangin' out here and there." And John was in the room, John Lennon. And he said, "Well, why don't you come out and stay at my place?" He had just acquired that place called Tittenhurst Park in Surrey,

I think it was, or Buckingham. Yeah. John Lennon's estate. And so, we went out to live with John. He gave the servants quarters over to us.

And by this time Prabhupada was really anxious to come to England. So, he came there and he stayed out at Tittenhurst Park. We picked him up in the airport in the Apple limousine. The big white Rolls. (Laughter) And running out there and the first thing; John and Yoko and George came to see him. That was there first meeting and that's all recorded. We have somewhere the text of that meeting. And Prabhupada was so charming and so alluring and so friendly that he just captivated everyone. Especially George.

GEORGE'S SONGS

And then George used to visit Prabhupada there quite frequently. And each time George came he just sat there, he asked a few simple questions, but mostly he just listened. And Prabhupada taught him all of the ancient secrets of existence. In this very encapsulated form, very simply put. So that George just absorbed this knowledge and began writing songs right away. You know like a few days later a song would pop out of his head that said just what Prabhupada had told him. That's when you have all these wonderful songs that appeared in "All Things Must Pass." That was the first album that reflected Prabhupada's philosophy and then later in '73, "Living in the Material World" which is all Krsna conscious philosophy almost a hundred percent.

One day he calls me up and he says he had been living in this small house in Eshire, but he wanted something bigger. He said, "Come on! Look at this old monastery I found" And he picked me up and we went out and looked at what has now become Friar Park. But in those days it was a nunnery and there were like about three or four nuns left in this huge 100 room castle and it was all run down. And the grounds were full with ivy and brambles. And he says, "I can get this for so much." I forgot how many pounds it was. "Do you think I should get it?" "Wow! this would be great George." So, he got it. He bought it and he asked me to come and live there with a few devotees to help him clean the grounds and get it cleaned up a bit. So I did.

This is kind of a funny story. One night they were all at Abby Road. We were all at Abby Road where they were recording one of the songs. I forget what it was. Maybe it was the last album, Some guy was up in the sky-light like this, above the studio. It was about that high too. Way up in the ceiling in this large studio room. And they were all playing something and (makes crashing sound) this guy fell through the glass and hit the piano and then onto the floor. And he was wearing like a sari—some nutcase. (laughter) And John's just playing along and he looks over like this, at this guy laying there and he looks up at George and he says, "Must be one of yours George," (laughter) and just kept playing.

HARSH WORDS

We never really had any harsh words, except once. I worked in the house a lot because it was raining and it was cold and wet that winter at Friar Park. We all lived in this hundred room house, even George and Patty in sleeping bags. There was no furniture. No heat. It was all being worked on gradually, but George was so busy with other things that not much was getting done in the way of developing the place. So we decided to develop the kitchen first. A huge kitchen as a center of comfort where it would be warm and everything would be nice, so we could all hang out in the kitchen. So one morning I was scraping the old fireplace there, taking off decades of Victorian paint off this beautiful fireplace. Big fireplace. And George came in and he was kinda sullen about something. He usually worked at night in the studios and he'd come in the mornings when we'd all be getting up and starting our work. And he'd always head for the kitchen and he was real sullen about something. I've forgotten entirely about what it was about. But he started making some… I was up on a ladder, he started making some very critical remarks. Something like, "You know, I don't know about your spiritual master. You know I, blah blah blah." And he started putting Krsna down and the spiritual master down, finding fault with this and finding fault with that. Finally I just came off that ladder at him and I shoved him real hard up against the wall. It looked like I was gonna slug him, I guess. And he got like this too (makes fist) and then we both just kinda went (sound of laughter) and broke up in laughter. It almost came to blows.

MY SWEET LORD

He would quite often come in with his rock n' roll side band, you know, after an all night session. I talked with Billy Preston, yesterday about this. He remembered too. So they came in all uproarious and boisterous and there was an organ in the kitchen. So Billy came in and he sat down behind the organ and Jim Keller set up his drums or something. You know they had some instruments and they got a little amp, plugged it in and they started. They said they wanted me to hear some song they'd been working on all night. They said that, "We're gonna call it 'My Sweet Lord'" (laughter) and the chorus was "halleluiah" and then I started shouting, "Hare Krsna, Hare Krsna" (sings in place of halleluiah) and then they began to join in on Hare Krsna and so we wound up with a mixture of both.

It had an amazing effect throughout the world. The young people… if the Beatles liked it then it's OK. Then it's OK. It's acceptable. Then they'd at least listen and then they had to make a decision if it was for them or not. But so many people did listen. Thousands. That was George's service to Prabhupada. In his visits to Prabhupada also, he was curious about whether he should don the robes, shave his head and wear the… you know. So, Prabhupada said, "No. Don't even become my initiated disciple. You are already my disciple. You are my son." And George mastered the art of talking about Krsna without mentioning Krsna, almost. He talked about God and cosmic consciousness and that kind of thing. He used those words. Got the message through. That song (sings) "Got a lot of work to do. Trying to get a message through." And his way of doing it was particularly unique and it was troubling to him how to do it, but eventually he felt comfortable with it. His preaching style he developed. Many of his songs have Krsna as the theme, but you don't know it.

Like when we first met. He and Patty went down to Sicily, a vacation, and he called me up one night in that little flat in Bitterton Street where it was so cold and said, "Syamasundara. I want to sing you this little ditty I just cooked up to see what you think—if anybody'll like it." And he sang (sings) "Here comes the sun, da da dada Here comes the sun." He sort of felt like Krsna was entering his life at that point. The things he was pulling out of, all this depressed period of the Beatles break-up and all that. And maybe other things, they had money problems and stuff. With all this lawyers and managers and people were screwing him and then he felt like "Here comes the sun" now. Krsna is telling me how to live and its all right now. And then "Something" song. The definition of Krsna is the all-attractive Supreme Personality. So George transformed that (sings) "attracts me like no other lover." And he told me later... He says, "I had to say 'she' Syamasundara. Otherwise they'd all think I'm a poof." (Laughter)

While I was gone, George put out "Living in the Material World" in the spring of '73. And the proceeds or part of the proceeds from that record and that album, he bought this huge estate for the Hare Krsna's out in Hertsfordshire which was called in those days Piggots Manor and we call it Bhaktivedanta Manor now. And Prabhupada came several times to Bhaktivedanta Manor, stayed long periods of time. Very nice house, big house. Not as big as George's, but very nice in the old manor style on 17 acres of land, really close to London. So George would come out to visit Prabhupada there also. So that their relationships continue, whether I was there or not. I came with Prabhupada in '73 and so on with George. And I brought George out a couple of times and he continued to visit on his own over the years.

GEORGE IN HIS LAST DAYS

In '99 I was in London for the summer so I got a good chance to rub elbows again with George and catch up things...

Interviewer: Did you notice any changes in him... or...

Yes! He was becoming so serene and so transcendental in his every action. You know, he was really making spiritual advancement. I was envious. He was much more spiritually advanced than I think I'll ever be. His outlook on the world was completely resigned to 'whatever Krsna wants. I'm ready. I've done everything. I've seen everything. I have no more attraction to this material world. I love everyone, but if Krsna calls me— I'll be happy."

Then we were here during the last days. There was no change so it was bright and full of color and his eyes were focused. He was totally conscious of Krsna. Right up to the end.

Interviewer: So were you here by coincidence or were you called or...?

Yeah. Olivia asked us to come over. I don't really want to talk about the last days to respect the privacy of their family. Their only statement has been "he was fully conscious of God. He was afraid of nothing and he was at peace with everything and that sums it up."

Well, George said that he felt that he had a few soul mates in this lifetime that he's traveled with along many trails, and past lives. Ravi and Bob Dylan and he even included me in that category. How undeserving as I am, I'll never be able to do justice to George's affection.

Yesterday there was a nice meeting of many old friends of Georges and it was nice seeing them all.

Interviewer: Where was that?

I don't know if they want me to talk about it even. It hasn't been in the press or anything yet. They may just want to keep it quiet. The ceremony was at the Lakeshrine at the SRF on Sunset. The chapel there. It felt very fitting enough to send off. And everyone was laughing and full of cheer because we all know... everyone knew George, and this includes some very famous and big people in this world, are absolutely convinced he's where he wants to be right now. George was always were he wants to be. And he is with Krsna now. George wrote the song "The Art of Dying" in 1969. Just dig up the lyrics of that, refresh yourself on that. He already knew back then.

He says:

There will come a time when all of us must leave here
and nothing Sister Mary can do will keep me here with you.
There is nothing in this life that I've been trying
to equal or surpass the art of dying.
There will come a time when all your hopes are fading,
when things it seems are very strange and have an awkward pain.
Searching for the truth among the lying
and answered when you've learned the art of dying.

This is 1969. Every time we met it was just like we just stopped the conversation a few minutes before and just picked it up again. This was no different. I just pray that when I leave this body I would pick it up again.

GEORGE HARRISON PRESS INTERVIEW

George: Well, I think everything in this world is improbable. You know like Shakespeare says the world is a stage and the people are its actors. In a way we are the audience and we are the performers on the stage of life. And, you know, there isn't anything you can think of that can't happen. There's nothing you can do that can't be done. And it's like that. So, to me, I think its just another beautiful part of the play. You know, it' like God makes up this incredible play and we all just act out the parts.

Interviewer: And so "All Things Must Pass" is only the title, the title is your motto?

George: Well it's not my motto. It's what exists. They say, "past has gone, thou canst not that recall. Future is not. May not be at all. Present is." You know, the only thing that exists is really the now. Just think. We're on television forever. (laughter)

Interviewer: All things must pass means everything will be finished?

George: That is all things must pass just shows the nature of the physical world. Everything is changing all the time. We get born and we die, but we are in this body and we go through from birth to death. We stay the same. The soul is the same, but the body is changing. And like that, you know, it's the nature of—it's called duality. And it just keeps changing, but everything passes except the essence of that, which is our soul.

Musically, I'm not really that good. I'm nowhere near on, you know, any level that's worth talking much about, musically. What I can do is like somebody who can make a cake. I can mix little things together, and shove a few apples in it, and put some icing on the top and make something that is quite nice. But, if you take it all apart, you know, I don't believe I have great musical ability or great lyrical ability. And I have a bigger problem than that— because of my influence from Indian music and that whole spiritual thing, I don't see the point to writing those songs like most people will write. I can write hundreds of songs, you know, "Hey baby whatcha gonna do." I can churn them out, but I don't want to. If I'm gonna say something, I'd like it to have some kind of importance, some value so that, you know, in twenty years time it's not just some dumb song that made some, you know, some royalties.

I mean the royalties are nice, but it would be good to be able to have something a little deeper. That's why the chants of India are much better, because it's all there in Sanskrit. You just say the Sanskrit and all mantras and all prayers have a spiritual connection. It's much easier than trying to write in English some incredible philosophy or something that has a value.

Swami Bhaktivedanta who started the Hare Krishna movement—he once said that he was the servant of the servant of the servant of God. So I mean what does that make me? I'm the servant of the servant of the servant of the servant of the servant. You know, we all have a duty and I mean that's the thing, being able to recognize when something is a duty as well as a pleasure.

Interviewer: Are you disillusioned?

George: You know I'm unhappy about the world being concreted over and all the forests chopped down and the air polluted and the fact the planet is in the control of mad people. You know, people who are crazy, people who are greedy, all these people who are selling the rainforests, you know, any forest. Just selling it because they make some money. I'm very unhappy about that. But I have a long-term view which is all things must pass. I mean, before it used to be "maybe they're gonna blow us up with H-bombs." But even that I thought, "It don't really matter. They can't destroy what's within ourselves." Krsna says, "there's no time when we didn't exist and there'll be no time when we will cease to exist." The only thing that changes is the body. So even if they blow us up with H-bombs our soul will stay in our other astral body and the only thing that won't be here is physical. So, you know, I'm sad about the world, but I look at it from within and without. (George Harrison Tribute Video; ITV)

WORDS FROM APPLE

(from the Introduction to the Krishna Book by George Harrison)

Everybody is looking for Krishna.

Some don't realize that they are, but they are.

KRISHNA is GOD, the source of all that exists, the Cause of all that is, was, or ever will be.

As GOD is unlimited, HE has many Names.

Allah-Buddha-Jehovah-Rama: ALL are KRISHNA, all are ONE.

God is not abstract; He has both the impersonal and the personal aspects to His personality which is SUPREME, ETERNAL, BLISSFUL, and full of KNOWLEDGE. As a single drop of water has the same qualities as an ocean of water, so has our consciousness the qualities of GOD'S consciousness, but through our identification and attachment with material energy (physical body, sense pleasures, material possessions, ego, etc.) our true

TRANSCENDENTAL CONSCIOUSNESS has been polluted, and like a dirty mirror it is unable to reflect a pure image.

With many lives our association with the TEMPORARY has grown. This impermanent body, a bag of bones and flesh, is mistaken for our true self, and we have accepted this temporary condition to be final.

Through all ages, great SAINTS have remained as living proof that this non-temporary, permanent state of GOD CONSCIOUSNESS can be revived in all living Souls. Each soul is potentially divine.

Krishna says in Bhāgavata Gita: "Steady in the Self, being freed from all material contamination, the yogi achieves the highest perfect ional stage of happiness in touch with the Supreme Consciousness. " (VI, 28)

YOGA (a scientific method for GOD (SELF) realization) is the process by which we purify our consciousness, stop further pollution, and arrive at the state of Perfection, full KNOWLEDGE, full BLISS.

If there's a God, I want to see Him. It's pointless to believe in something without proof, and Krishna Consciousness and meditation are methods where you can actually obtain GOD perception. You can actually see God, and hear Him, play with Him. It might sound crazy, but He is actually there, actually with you.

There are many yogic Paths-Raja, Janna, Hath, Kraal, Karma, Bhakti-which are all acclaimed by the MASTERS of each method.

SWAMI BHAKTIVEDANTA is as his title says, a BHAKTI Yogi following the path of DEVOTION. By serving GOD through each thought, word and DEED, and by chanting HIS Holy Names, the devotee quickly develops God-consciousness. By chanting

Hare Krishna, Hare Krishna
Krishna Krishna, Hare Hare
Hare Rama, Hare Rama
Rama Rama, Hare Hare

One inevitable arrives at KRISHNA Consciousness. (The proof of the pudding is in the eating!)I request that you take advantage of this book KRISHNA, and enter into its understanding. I also request that you make an appointment to meet your God now, through the self liberating process of YOGA (UNION) and GIVE PEACE A CHANCE.

(hand written)

All you need is Love (Krishna) Hari Bol.
George Harrison 31/3/70

Apple Corps Ltd 3 Savile Row London W1 Gerrard 2771/3993 Telex Apcore London

His Holiness Tamal Krishna Goswami Maharaja (1946-2002), was accepted as a disciple by His Divine Grace A.C. Bhaktivedanta Swami Prabhupada in 1968, he quickly emerged as a leader in ISKCON, establishing temples around the world. As one of Srila Prabhupada's most trusted disciples, he often served as Srila Prabhupada personal secretary. He served on ISKCON's Governing Body Commission since its inception in 1970. In January 1972, he accepted the renounced order of life (sannyasa) from his spiritual master, A. C. Bhaktivedanta Swami Prabhupada in Jaipur, India. He served as ISKCON's first GBC Secretary for India from 1970-74 and was appointed trustee of the Bhaktivedanta Book Trust, responsible for U.S. sales. In 1977, he served as Srila Prabhupada's last personal secretary. Since that time, he served as the GBC Secretary for Texas and a large number of countries in the Orient. His publications include: Reason and Belief: Problem-solving in the Philosophy of Religion (Pundits Press, 1997); Yoga for the 21st Century (1991); Prabhupada Antya-lila: The final Pastimes of Srila Prabhupada (Washington, D.C.: Institute for Vaishnava Studies, 1988); Jagannatha-Priya-Natakam: The Drama of Lord Jagannatha (Cambridge, Massachusetts: Bhaktivedanta Institute of Religion and Culture, 1985); and Servant of the Servant (Hong Kong: BBT, 1984). He initiated around a thousand disciples and was responsible for bringing many thousands of souls into Krishna consciousness.

Tamal Krishna Goswami's Disappearance Festival
The day after his departure March 16, 2002, Mayapur Dham

Jayapataka Swami...

Hare Krsna. Goes back a long way with us. When I joined in San Francisco I saw him there in the kirtana, so many wonderful inspiring devotees. In 1970 when I came to India then he was my GBC from '71 on. Srila Prabhupada made me Calcutta temple president. Tamal Krishna Goswami was my GBC to guide and check my service. He a perfectionist and I wasn't. So I was temple president there for 11 times. The record. Ten times he removed me. (laughter) Either the alternative was worse or Srila Prabhupada put me back.

Apart from that, he was a very kind friend. I was respectful as he was GBC, but when I came to Maypur, we worked as a team, dedicated to develop

Mayapur. In '77 I became co-GBC and we worked together. When I was in the intensive care unit of the hospital in 1989 after nearly dying he came to the hospital to see me with Sivarama Swami and Sivarama Swami's Gaur Nitai. Then I had no thread so I asked him to chant on a thread for me so it would be in parampara and he did it. Yesterday I saw he had no thread so I did the same to him, as he would have wanted one.

I'm grateful to him for coming. He was about to get his PHD . . .. and going to work on the Mayapur Project. Gave a lot of input in the meeting. The Lord has His inconceivable plan. Tamal Krishna Goswami is with Srila Prabhupada certainly. I'm sure they'll make plans for these projects.

Yesterday we rushed to the site, horrible to see the car. The local people said only injured nobody was so badly hurt. I was sure Krsna would allow him to survive since there is so much service to do.

Phuliya, where the accident occurred, is part of the Dhama where Haridas Thakur used to chant his three lakhs of names. It is associated with Haridas Thakur. So Tamal Krishna Goswami was doing all these kirtans this last week and it significant that he left there.

We got there and they told us he had gone. We were overwhelmed. Then they told us she is still alive. I was trying get her shifted to Calcutta. Danavir Maharaja was chanting and Sivarama Swami and Bhakti Bhrnga Maharaja were consoling the disciples and Jayadvaita Swami was helping me. Incredibly intense situation.

When we put them in the vehicle about 300 people blocked us and said they were waiting to see the saint, and wouldn't let us go. So we had to show them. They were lying in front of the tire. When they saw him they spontaneously chanted. This the first time everyone in Shantipur was chanting, they normally have a reputation to be inimical to Vaisnavas.

His loss is incalculable. He touched so many people. He was wise, loyal, devoted, aristocratic and Krsna and Prabhupada-conscious. He trained disciples who are such an asset. Promoting ISKCON as a family and who would hold it together. He lives with all us by his teachings, the mission of Srila Prabhupada and we have his footsteps to follow in. This is a test, now we have to surrender to his vani. After the nice training he gave you I'm sure you'll be wonderful examples. We hope to support you in this time of need. He had such a high standard with his blessings you can follow.

Once I met disciple of Bhaktisiddhanta Sarasvati Thakur. He was one of the last disciples to be initiated. He made a song to glorify each of his Godbrothers. At that time there were only 6 left, how much separation he was feeling. Now Tamal Krishna Goswami has increased our realization of Godbrothers.

BB Govinda Maharaja's story made me feel bad as I thought Tamal Krishna Goswami so much above me. We did get a lot of association and consider him a dear friend and Godbrother. I'm sorry if I didn't reciprocate as much as I should have. Thank you for your association.

Keshava Bharati Prabhu...

Tamal Krishna Goswami, when I heard the news yesterday I could not conceive of how it would be for you possible to be in the car and run into a tree. You were so attentive to details. Our lives were intertwined. During Prabhupada's presence when I watched you, when I assisted you in serving him. How attentive you were.

All day yesterday I could only chant Hare Krishna and it was inconceivable. I only could conceive one thing that Prabhupada has called you back. I want to make it as short as I can because I can't speak. The essence of Tamal Krishna Goswami's heart was ecstatic love for Srila Prabhupada. Wherever he went before and after disappearance of Srila Prabhupada he always had the murti of Srila Prabhupada.

You're not an ordinary person. You are a great soul. Great souls are never attracted to anything mediocre. They are driven by energies that are very difficult to understand. I know that you're one of most misunderstood personalities that I met in my life. When Srila Prabhupada departed I was fortunate enough to be in the room and assist you in serving Srila Prabhupada during those days. When Srila Prabhupada departed the world became vacant.

Externally Srila Prabhupada used you to keep you, to use you with very deep intelligence and organize things to push Krishna consciousness from one place to another form San Francisco, to India, China, etc. He used you as an instrument because you wanted to ...

Some people, please forgive me for mentioning this. Some people have actually criticized him for not crying when Srila Prabhupada left this world .. how could he have the ecstatic love for Srila Prabhupada when he was so unmoved ... But the next day when we took Srila Prabhupada on his flower airplane around Vrndavana, he was fanning Srila Prabhupada and I was next to him. I was watching very carefully and tears started to shoot from his eyes, that it knocked his glasses off and he couldn't put them back on. At that moment I knew I was watching someone with ecstatic love for Srila Prabhupada.

I could go on the whole day to explain so many things, but I want to say that in all the years that we were together when our relationship became so interesting that sometimes it became too hard to take, I would go and come back... And at some point I realized that I was being trained in a way that was inconceivable, and I was trained by a person who was trained like that by Srila Prabhupada. I eternally indebted to you for the training that you gave me, for opportunities of service, for introducing me to Srila Prabhupada. I am going to miss you a lot, a lot... He was so intelligent and so organized and I don't know.. somehow or other some different kinds of things that were... I pray to be able to be serve Srila Prabhupada with you as soon as possible. It's not possible to explain it with any words.. it's inconceivable.

Giridhari Swami...

It's difficult to speak in these circumstances, I was very shocked on getting the news. I had the great fortune from the beginning of my live in Krsna consciousness to have his association many places, times, various types of service, and I witnessed a great unceasing determination to serve Srila Prabhupada, through each and every activity he did. Many qualities we could focus, main is his determination to spread Krishna consciousness and overcome all obstacles. Particularly from when we went to Hong Kong in 1980.

In those days it was still British, but had tremendous restrictions and Krishna consciousness hadn't blossomed there. So from beginning he worked very hard to re-establish, worked with lawyers, had to grow hair, get the society re-registered, just to lay the groundwork. No local devotees and we tried to conceive how to spread through yoga in an undercover way. A number of those attracted by yoga became our first devotees, and then we were able to do harināma, books, and all other outreach programs.

From 1987 we were inspired by Kirtiraja Prabhu to try to do more in China. Up till then it was closed and one could hardly get a visa for more than a few days. But then opportunity arose, so inspired by him Tamal Krishna Goswami said "now or never. Let's try". He was feeling the push of Srila Prabhupada to do something bigger. We were bold, in devotional attire and did harināma sitting in parks for hours. Hundreds of people were attracted, surrounding us, inquisitive about us. In between the chanting he would speak with a translator, and attracted people, the first devotees. We kept on, then couldn't continue in that way, and again we went undercover, but this was the foundation. From that time we had number of devotees in various places, participating in Krishna consciousness. He inspired it, worked tirelessly all day, working working. How to organize better, improve, engage others, delegate, use time best way... I witnessed all my devotional life with him that he was tremendously determined. Others would give up, he would overcome obstacles. Extraordinary. He was very kind personally though I didn't deserve it. He went out of way to inspire, encourage, train, give me responsibility. Always pushing me forward. Sometimes against my conditioned will but he knew how to get the most out of me. It was hard as I am limited, but later when I thought about it I saw he was always correct in his perceptions. What to do, how he trained me to do properly. Eternally indebted. From beginning to present, will go on for every breath of this life to render service to him and disciples and followers. I pray that together we'll be able realize his dreams in various projects and please Srila Prabhupada in the way he strived to.

Ekacakra Prabhu...

(One of the devotees responsible for preaching in China.)

So I have had quite extensive association with HH Tamal Krishna Goswami in the preaching of Krishna consciousness in China. And just to illustrate a couple of the qualities he had I would like to relate some incidents from our preaching. As Giridhari Swami said just how Tamal Krishna Goswami was such a determined preacher.

Once in China in 1988, there was no devotees so we used to attend English corners: gatherings of Chinese practising English together. We'd go there and start speaking. Find some way to preach to them. I remember once he in one hour could speak to someone who had no idea about Krishna consciousness, present them the whole philosophy in an easy and concise way. Take them to the hotel, feed them vegetarian Chinese prasadam. Some of them on the spot, everything first time, they would surrender and ask "What now?" Then he told them the 4 regs, 16 rounds and they started from the first day they met him. This is one aspect. Expert, forceful preacher.

Another aspect is his kind gentle nature. He appears heavy, but actually gentle and kind. I remember once in China the first time I cooked. I wasn't very experienced. He told us to buy vegetarian cooking books so the locals would relate and become vegetarian. I had no experience, and we know that to cook for him one has to be together.

Every five minutes he was checking me. I was nervous. I managed a few subjis, rice, soup. I was serving but he told me to eat together with him. This was all in the hotel room. The kitchen was on the desk, the bathroom was for washing. Then he got up went to the bathroom, washed and came out and asked what he could serve me. I was a 6-month bhakta and he was serving me. I was embarrassed but accepted. As Kesava Bharati Prabhu said, he was one of the most misunderstood devotees, but I can assure you from my experience that nobody was more kind than him. So today I pray I become a perfect tool for preaching Krishna consciousness in China and a pure servant of HH Tamal Krishna Goswami and the acaryas, and develop the strength and humility to serve the Vaisnavas properly.

Jahnava devi dasi...

(Wife of Ekacakra and translator of Srila Prabhupada's books in Chinese. Speaks in Chinese with Ekacakra translating in English)

I don't know what urgent matter Krsna has to take away Guru Maharaja so suddenly. To me this just like thunder striking in clear weather. Sad experience. Not feeling sad for him so much because he has gone to Srila Prabhupada and Krsna and is happy with them. Now I feel so much regret, tortured by regret. Krsna was so merciful to give me such a merciful Guru

Maharaja but I didn't properly treasure it. I first saw him 8 years ago, initiated 6 years ago. Since then he was always so merciful to me. But I wasn't properly reciprocating and grateful enough. So fallen, he wanted me to take the elevator to Krsna but I was struggling with his mercy. To take diksa is in one sense a formal ceremony. But to try to do according to the guru's heart's desire isn't so easy.

So in process of trying to serve him and be of one mind, I had 4 stages. Today I tell this in front of the Taiwanese devotees so they don't make the same mistakes at initiation. I speak in front of Radha Madhava, Srila Prabhupada, and all devotees in a confession so I can be relieved from the bottom of my heart. From the first day he gave me strong pressure. Then I was distributing books in China. He said, "I wanted to have a disciple in China who can do 100 Gitas a day". Then I was doing books for 8-9 hours, and do 30-40 at most. When I heard this I thought "This is impossible, I'll be spitting blood to do 100!" Then a devotee saw my doubt and came to me: "When guru gives instruction he also gives the power to accomplish it. Try your best to follow then you'll be successful." I didn't understand but tried. After 2 months, miracle happened. After 6 hours of book distribution, I had done 70 books. Then I went home tired. I thought "I did 70 in 6 hours, a little more then I could do 100." Next day I did a bit longer and did 90 books, 3rd day more than 100.

(Clapping, Haribol)

(Choking) – not my own strength, Krsna was pleasing Guru Maharaja through me. Then I went to meet him in Hong Kong and he gave me his own murti of Lord Caitanya. He also gave me his chadar. But I was such a neophyte and hard-hearted and I didn't appreciate this. Then after initiation he told me translate in Chinese. He wanted all Srila Prabhupada's books in Chinese in his lifetime and I couldn't do it. And in process of translation, some incident happened. These things are Krsna's tests to me but then I was stubborn and didn't understand. Guru Maharaja so wise, so experienced in management so when he considers something he does it best.

I was stubbornly attached to my idea thinking I was right and others wrong. Even though he spent money to fly devotees to the Phillipines to speak to me, he talked on the phone for one hour from America but still I failed. I was not submissive so my heart became harder. Even up to the point that I thought he didn't understand me, and I didn't want to see him anymore. Later by my husband's mercy I met many senior Vaisnavas and realized my mistake. Then I felt I was so dirty, unfit to appear in front of Guru Maharaja. When I had the chance to meet him I hid and tried to avoid his association.

This happened till about 6 months ago when we met him in Hong Kong. He personally said we now have to establish with full trust a father and daughter relationship. He said if you fully surrender then you will have no more anxiety or worry.

Then I did as he said. And I finally started tasting the guru-disciple sweet relationship only for half a year. Just when I started to get it, Krsna took him away. So human beings are like this, they don't treasure something till they lose it. Now I don't know what to do.

If I do something right who will encourage and praise me? If I do something wrong, who will mercifully and lovingly chastise me like he did? And when I doubt and hesitate who will help me with the right decision? The only solace is that this time he has seen so many devotees from Taiwan, which gave him so much happiness and satisfaction. This was his greatest wish and desire to have all Chinese people accept Krishna consciousness. It was the instruction he received from his own spiritual father. I have an unrepayable debt to him. So I can only try best to do some service for him. So he may be pleased and come in front of me again one day. (Applause)

Abhiram Prabhu...

Tamal Krishna Goswami has been my dearest friend and brother since a long time. The most unusual relationship and combination of people. We are as different as oil and water. I didn't have any intention to love him but instantly I did. I met him in 1974. And from then on our relationship was intense, moving, efficacious, inspiring, challenging, annoying, disturbing, but always always causing growth, increasing love. Tamal Krishna Goswami was a Vaisnava, a personalist, not a cultish— not singular in dimension, he was multi-faceted. Like chutney: hot and sweet at the same time. Always loving. Not love that is understood materially. Not always sugary. But always inspiring.

A few words, this not cohesive, but here are a few comments: One of most profound aspects of my association with him was the sense of family. I think you all have some experience of seeing him, speaking, sharing prasadam, or your heart with him. Whoever touched him came into his family and remained there. This was not an issue of convenience. God knows in my case he pulled me out of the gutter a number of times, I didn't ask or welcome him, but he did it. Now I can just be eternally grateful.

Impossible: He loved the challenge of the impossible and demanded it from us and got it. Obtained it. He tasted every type of joy and sublime rasa that a disciple of Srila Prabhupada could be expected to taste in this lifetime. One thing eluded him, as I know him, and I pray he has that now, and that is peace. I pray (choking) I know his connection with Srila Prabhupada and Krsna is only deeply intensified with the death of the body. That which drove him which kept him up and annoyed him, that desire to unite I'm sure he has found that. Perfect union. Or will do so very shortly.

Last word: Grief. I was with a very dear Godsister Kusa on the way to Vrndavana when I heard

the news. And I began crying, vomiting, convulsing. She said I should take some time out to grieve, but I had a different view. We grieve for those of this world whom we love or share, to let them go, release them and us from that pain. That grief should be engaged and dispensed and we go on. But the grief for a devotee becomes a part of us, moulds us, ennobles, drives us, it's not to be dispensed with, it beautifies the soul. So the Vaisnavas pray "I bang my head, no hope." But this grief drives us toward that spiritual world where the departed Vaisnavas reside. This is the proof that a Vaisnava is on thee Absolute platform because even in grieving for him we get encouraged, strengthened, find our way forward. I think you will all know very well about this point.

So I suggest this is a grief we should embrace positively since he was a Vaisnava, a contradictory person from a mundane point of view, always driving us, always loving us— maintaining his family and expanding it selflessly, indiscriminatingly, not just ISKCON devotees, or Godbrothers, or men. . . .

Vaisnava Gosai ki jai!

Niranjana Swami...

Boston Gaur Nitai installation in 1976. He was doing the installation and came to me and asked me to please sing this melody for the whole installation. It was two hours long. Then he said this is my favorite tune. So I thought I would take the opportunity to chant it for him; last week we were chanting together, he was relishing it, remembering this as his favorite melody. So I chant it for his pleasure today. (Kirtana for 15 minutes)

Visvambhar Prabhu...

(Disciple of Tamal Krishna Goswami)

The night before, he asked me to come upstairs and sat me down nicely. He said I would like to have your association though I am packing. And he was packing just like a baby. I was observing every single movement and I said "Oh you are very neat and clean and very organized. He said, "Yes Visvambhar I got this training from my mother. She is German. Tomorrow I'm going back home, right?" That's what he said, and I stopped, and assumed he meant home. "Oh, you like the home in England." Then he smiled. And then he was asking me some advice of what to do with some rupees that he had in his drawer. What to do? Either to take them to England or leave them here. It's illegal to take them out of India, I told him. "Yes I won't need." Then Naresvara Prabhu and Bhakti Purusottama Swami came. I know he likes to be with his Godbrothers, he said Srila Prabhupada left him only this wealth. So I was just about to leave, saying goodbye. Then he told me "You go to the Ganga and my pay my last obeisances, bathe and represent me." I though last meant of this trip, but then the next morning. . .

He was so excited while packing like a child going from boarding school to see his parents. I feel he was expecting to go. I think he knew. I remember in UK when he invited us to Christmas Dinner, along with Kesava Bharati our very dear uncle, he invited my family: "Don't serve, go to Kesava Bharati Prabhu and bring him and we'll all sit as a family. He sat at head, your uncle there, you as son sit here with your wife and kids on other side. We were eating, he said "this is very family-like, this like the last supper. It looks like the Last Supper." We had a toast like karmis, with a drink. Hold a cup with grape juice, and wished. His wish was "I hope everyone goes back to Godhead soon."

All these indications. Last supper with my father. Ganga pranam on his behalf. He also said "I'm going back home tomorrow" I think he knew he was going. Pure devotees know Krsna's plan and guru's. But act like conventional. But I felt him very enthusiastic. He wanted me to come to Mayapur when he was there. He wanted to give me these 15 days, I got deep realizations with him in kirtana and with his Godbrothers. About his affection to disciples and everyone. I finish here. I just want to say please all of you kindly, goduncles, godaunts, godcousins, to look upon us very mercifully. A great loss, very sad, we need to be kept in your mercy.

I was supposed to be there in the car with him. My train was 5pm so I told him I don't know what to do in Calcutta for 6 hours so I'll take a taxi at 12pm. I feel very sad and just like the senior devotees said we have to take shelter of the holy name and senior Vaisnavas. So my duty as Godbrother is to ask all of you to kindly don't give up your determination or inspiration of your spiritual master and take association of his Godbrother and Godsisters who were his only family. Thank you very much, Hare Krsna.

Radhanatha Swami…

The first time I met His Divine Grace Tamal Krishna Maharaja was in March 1971 in Bombay. It was Srila Prabhupada's first major large scale programme in India with tens of thousands of people. I was asked to sit close to Srila Prabhupada on the stage. There was kirtan, he spoke from Srimad Bhagavatam, and at then end when he was leaving he walked in front of me. I went to touch his feet, just then Tamal Krishna Maharaja thundered: "No-one touches Srila Prabhupada's feet!" I was fearful and retreated. I thought it was an offence. Srila Prabhupada smiled and said to me "You can touch my feet." (laughter)

Next in Vrndavana in November 1971. Srila Prabhupada would give afternoon darshan and then the devotees would do sankirtan. I came from the Himalayas with long matted hair, not a devotee yet. So Tamal Krishna Goswami saw me sitting with Srila Prabhupada. And said: "All devotees must go out on sankirtana, no sitting here." I showed him my locks and said I was not devotee. And Srila Prabhupada said to him also "He is not a devotee let him stay". (laughter)

This was Tamal Krishna Goswami. He didn't concern himself with popularity. Just to serve the order of his Guru Maharaja. Srila Prabhupada told him what to do, "don't let anyone touch my feet", etc. Srila Prabhupada saw in him one who would do anything at the risk of his life, so he could entrust him with things that nobody else in the world could do.

Srila Prabhupada wanted land in Mayapur, all the other devotees failed to get it. Then Srila Prabhupada sent Tamal Krishna Goswami. Brahmananda told me that Srila Prabhupada sent Tamal Krishna Goswami because no-one else could do it. It was against all odds, would take weeks, almost impossible. After great efforts he did it and returned to Calcutta at night. He came in to Srila Prabhupada's room: "I was waiting for you". Maharaja gave him the deed: "The land is yours!" Srila Prabhupada said, "Thank you very much, now you can take rest."

He told me the most hard service was to publish the first Krsna book in Japan. A whole story in itself. Srila Prabhupada used him to do impossible things. When the books came to India Srila Prabhupada wanted it for the pandal programme. But there was strike at the docks. Violent criminals were lined up to block, and beat and kill anyone who tried to enter. But Srila Prabhupada wanted the books. What would you do? He [Tamal Krishna Maharaja] went to all ministers, they told him no-one can get through, it's impossible. He went to Delhi, he would not accept that it's impossible. Srila Prabhupada demonstrated this principle through him. Eventually some very big minister signed a paper, then he went from office to office in Calcutta. In the end he did it, had all the books to be distributed.

He was Temple President in Los Angeles. Top temple in world. Then he went to London, Srila Prabhupada called him there to enliven the preaching. Then he did it there, then Prabhupada called him to India to enliven the preaching. As Kesava Bharati Prabhu said he was unpopular sometimes as he didn't care for himself, he only wanted to execute the instructions of Srila Prabhupada, so all who love Srila Prabhupada must be eternally indebted to him... Of all leaders Srila Prabhupada wanted him by his side the most and had full faith in his surrender. If we keep his example and follow then we also become dear to Srila Prabhupada and Radha Madhava.

Tamal Krishna Goswami Ki jai!

Gaur-Narayana Prabhu...

So Guru Maharaja, His Divine Grace Tamal Krishna Maharaja has left us in the midst of the ocean of grief. Though he is not present still his vani is present forever with us. So Guru Maharaja has now accepted a permanent residence in our hearts . . . when he was present we would remember him sometimes and forget him sometimes, but now in separation we will always remember and try to follow.

Many of us had less association with Maharaja. They might feel alone, but on behalf of all of the Godbrothers I want to assure that all his disciples are never alone. The whole society is here to help them and guide in spiritual advancement. The way we saw yesterday how all came forward with love and consoled us and did all the correct activities for Guru Maharaja. So on behalf of all Godbrothers I express gratitude to all the devotees and God-uncles. Again this has proven that our society is in union and not dismantled.

So about my relationship with Guru Maharaja: He has been very affectionate and actually gave me residence at Giriraja. Once he wrote from Dallas that, "My dear Gaura Narayana, (sobbing) You are very fortunate to live there at Govardhan. But I am not so fortunate as for preaching I have to be away, so when I get qualified to live there I'll come". I wrote back, "You are the most qualified to live here, even if you are elsewhere your heart is here. I am not qualified, it is only your mercy that I am here, I have no qualification".

He told me that there your only service is to serve Giriraja and the devotees of ISKCON. So he got that project as a facility for the leaders and devotees so when they get tired from preaching outside, they can come and stay for a few days, do bhajans, parikrama and re-charge their batteries and enthusiasm. He made this facility for the whole society but he couldn't use it himself. He told me that after completing his thesis on Srila Prabhupada's contribution to the world, after that I'll come for 2 months. (Sobbing) I'll give you sannyasa there.

Once I was serving in Vrndavana, and when leaving I asked him "Gurudeva I have committed many offences while serving you. Please forgive me". He replied "You can't make any offence, by chastising you I made an offence. Please forgive me. I am doing it so you can serve in a perfect way. That was his mood in chastising us, to train us to be perfect devotees.

Many may misunderstand that he is so heavy, but his real mood is to train his duty as guru. He always instructed us to treat all Godbrothers as equal to me. He taught us like that. We will try to follow this, treat our uncles, and now take shelter of them. (Crying) Please excuse me, I can't speak any more. Hare Krsna.

Kalasamvara Prabhu...

(He was in the car with Tamal Krishna Maharaja and his wife, Srimate Vrindavaneswari devi dasi who also passed away in the same car accident.)

Hare Krsna. I don't know how people many are here as I don't have my glasses. Different people have different relations with Krsna, same with the devotees. My relationship with Tamal Krishna Goswami was based on friendship, and guidance. He didn't exhibit his power to me. We were in touch by email. Great relationship. He'll be missed in my life, like it will be for everyone. Friendships are very rare in this world. We should appreciate devotees before they leave, express this, as devotees are so rare. Now the whole ISKCON is disturbed by one Vaisnava's disappearance.

A devotee's life is like chapters, when do we judge a person as we haven't seen all the chapters? We'll always remember this Festival as he added the hariman kirtan which is what we are here for. To relish Lord Caitanya's and Nityananda's mellows. Srila Prabhupada said devotional service is an apprenticeship, to learn how to deal with the devotees on a higher level. . . If we believe Krsna, Tamal Krishna Goswami has finished his apprenticeship. He was so expert and intellectually strong. His lectures can take us where we want to go. I hope as life goes on my conviction will get stronger. I can't help but think that he has finished his apprenticeship. I have full conviction of that.

He never chastised me, had great feeling, and will be dearly missed. How do you replace this? For us it's sad, for him with Krsna, it's the greatest. So we should think of that, we all want that, if he is there then it is a joyful day to think of him.

So yesterday was an incredible experience. To lose one dear friend is hard, to lose two friends in one day I find pretty amazing. Both very dear to me. Such an incredible week. The ending has been more incredible. We had such a pleasant week, so loving and spiritual. According to Nectar of Devotion piety is if one can sing beautifully and has intelligence.

Tamal Krishna Goswami's kirtanas have been exemplary. We were discussing about the kirtanas with Visnujana. Tamal Krishna Goswami said the ones in the last week surpassed everything. This is potency. He said "I'm not chanting, just sitting here but all these devotees are coming and chanting."

Tamal Krishna Goswami and Vrindavaneswari had a nice relationship. Via email she would ask so many questions, and he could satisfy her intellect. It was her birthday yesterday. She wanted to ride with him in the airport. Some rumours had been going around about the political situation, so I joked that best we all go together so if there is any problem we can leave [this world?] together. I think it would be hard for her to survive without Tamal Krishna Goswami. Special that they went to go together. She did millions of dollars collection. Gave it all to ISKCON and her guru. If anyone needed she would send to them. She used to think "Why doesn't Krsna give more, we need to glorify Krsna more!" Laksmi and prasadam were here fortes. She is famous in New Zealand for this. She was making cakes here also. Even could do it here in India, could master the art. She could go in the kitchen and get something together immediately if anyone was hungry. Very giving, she would give so much of her time. Liked best to chant japa or kirtana. No matter when she slept she would go mangal-arati and chant her 16 rounds. Her hand was like this yesterday when she left her body as we were chanting (sobbing) her arm froze in that position. When the ladies were preparing the body, the rest was soft but her arm was hard. That's how she would be with her beads, chanting while swaying, Hare Krishna Hare Krishna Krishna Krishna Hare Hare / Hare Rama Hare Rama Rama Rama Hare Hare.

Another great loss to our society. A handful of rare devotees in the planet. Must be appreciated. So much sacrifice, we have no Krsna, Lord Caitanya or even Srila Prabhupada, so for people to come to us in Kali yuga is an amazing thing. We must let devotees know how much we appreciate them. It shouldn't come to the point that devotees leave without feeling appreciated.

Bhakti Tirtha Swami was happy that the devotees were praying for him during his operation. His comment was why should we not always pray for the devotees? . . . Many devotees are getting old, we have to care and look after devotees. She was always caring, she would take care of the widows here and in Vrndavana. She would give, she might have nothing and I would be annoyed when she gave whatever she got. Simple life.

Incredible day yesterday. I have to get myself together and find another shelter. To lose my dear wife and Maharaja has left a huge vacuum in my heart and mind. I don't know Krsna's plan. She always told me she wanted to die before me. In the same way I don't think she could survive Tamal Krishna Goswami's departure. Ultimate birthday present.

I got her a book about Radha Kund and Tamal Krishna Goswami wrote a nice note in it:

"To my dear Vrindavanesvari, I hope that by the grace of your spiritual masters you will attain spiritual fulfillment and residence on the banks of Radha Kunda."

She was disciple of Indradyumna Swami and took siksa from Tamal Krishna Goswami. The relationship was getting sweeter and sweeter. She wanted to also start these bhajan nights in New Zealand. Tamal Krishna Goswami was taking this to new heights. The devotees are incredible who can arouse these feelings, emotions in us. Just like the kirtan we just had. So much nectar, but we don't realize it.

I will always preach, especially this week's kirtanas were a manifestation of his potency, he came here after so long, incredible mood like no more distinctions of senior and junior—all just friends.

So take this mood back to your temples. Every place has a great singer and this should be part of our process. We should sit around at night and imbibe the mood of Krsna and have a picture of Tamal Krishna Goswami and maybe one of her too and dive into the nectar of Krsna.

As a wife, she was very dutiful, an incredible devotee that's why I wanted to take her association. . . . She couldn't find faults in ISKCON—just we need to do more kirtana and japa. This is one of the aspects of the Krishna consciousness movement.

I'll keep it short: Tamal Krishna Goswami ki jai!

BVV Narasimha Maharaja...

Before meeting Tamal Krishna Goswami I heard a lot about him. I saw him in 1974 in New York. He showed his beautiful etiquette of bringing silver presents for the deities, and holy water and dust. We can see how he was always very expert in dealing. He could handle all difficult things easily.

Later I joined him in the Phillipines, preaching together. Not easy to preach, Catholics, we were not big there. But he was able to meet Marcos, the President. And the cardinals, church heads, he would ask them, "Can you tell me about God's activities in the spiritual world?" "Oh, we don't know." He had 5 questions like that and they failed to answer any of them.

Then in China in '88. Srila Prabhupada could speak English in US, but we couldn't speak any Chinese when we went to China. Only Ekacakra could speak a little bit. "Impossible" was not a word in his [Tamal Krishna Maharaja's] dictionary.

After some time in China he said "Now I can see why Srila Prabhupada sent me here: these people know what discipline is!" China was good for him for that reason. We rented big presidential suites in hotels, and smuggled in gas and stoves, vegetables etc., then all the devotees would come for feast, kirtana, etc., and then they would kick us out. "We heard you are cooking and singing." "Who us, no!" Every city we did like this in different hotels. They don't give suites like that easily. That's how we preached.

I wrote to him when he went to Oxford: "Just as when Sarvabhauma Bhattacarya surrendered to Lord Caitanya all the other scholars also surrendered, in the same way I'm looking forward to seeing all scholars surrender to you." He thanked me for that.

I was blessed by these last 10 days. He seemed so peaceful here, nice chanting in kirtana with the devotees. He took the Taiwanese devotees to Srila Prabhupada's room and introduced them to him. "Now I've brought the Chinese devotees to you, Srila Prabhupada."

Lastly, he chose the best time and place to depart. If his samadhi was in Govardhan less of us would be able to go and see it. To have it here is wonderful. And during the festival so so many devotees could honour him. Krsna arranges his devotees to be glorified. He was used by Srila Prabhupada, others might say he used people, but he did so not for himself, only for Krsna and Srila Prabhupada.

Radha Krsna Prabhu...

(Disciple of Tamal Krishna Maharaja)

I can't speak loud, hard just to breathe. Nice to hear the glorification. Last time we met in Houston in November. Then Chaitanya Prabhu asked him if he could come to Mayapur when he would be there. He replied "No, I'll be busy, don't disturb me." So we planned to go elsewhere first, as if he saw us here he would be obligated to take care of us. So when he heard our plan he told Rtadhvaja Swami "What do you think of this? My disciples want to go to Vrindavana when I am in Mayapur!" When we heard this we told him, "But we didn't want to incontinence you!" "No, it's OK", was his reply. "But when you come here go with Sivarama Swami on parikrama." I served him since my first days in devotional service, in 1992. I was his personal secretary, servant, cook, I nursed him after the operation.

He was so merciful as you heard, and heavy too. I am a product of this. I've been shouted at, subjected to all types of treatment. Once he physically kicked me out, and I was doing my typing, and he buzzed me: "Do you know the spiritual master owns the body of the disciple?" He felt he might have hurt me, but I knew about the story of Lord Caitanya and Sanatana Goswami. I felt so wonderful that he was worried, and he was like that with everyone. Alert to other's feeling.

I am attentive to detail, but do you know the magnitude of his detailedness. He worships Srila Prabhupada murti exactly same way daily, shouldn't move anything in the wrong spot even an inch.

Once he asked me something and I gave another opinion. "You don't train me, I was trained by Srila Prabhupada! You get trained now!"

He was like chutney, hot and spicy but also sweet, intimate. Nine months ago our Godsister Kirtida died. He was there with her, held her hand, he was encouraging to remember Krsna, reading sastra, he arranged kirtana 24 hours so she could leave fully Krishna consciousness.

Then he could do anything. Once he had to go to college he had to go on the highway. We were bothered by the traffic lights. Every time it would go red, when we approached it wasn't a smooth flow. He said to call the traffic authority so he could go smoothly and so could all others. We did that, called the traffic department and they agreed!

I saw him learn harmonium. In minutes he picked it up. No paperwork or notes, I was amazed. He doesn't waste a second. Even while sleeping he'd wake up with dreams about Srila Prabhupada and serving Srila Prabhupada with his Godbrothers.

Sweet, but if we made mistakes then blasted us. Very sweet. Those who didn't see him close have missed this opportunity. He was very fond of his Godbrothers and would always call them for any decision he had to make: "This is what I want to do, what do you think?" He would even ask us. While he was typing letters he would ask my advice.

He was a dear friend constant guide. Always training. He said Srila Prabhupada entrusted him with the movement and nothing should go wrong with it, so he was attentive to every detail so there would be no deviation. He would chastise then check if we were OK. When we cry, he'd say, "Don't cry. If you cry the fun is over."

He wasn't a meanie. Sometimes he would tell me "Go back to your country!" Then he would call me to massage him. Just to pacify me he would change the subject. Always concerned and worried about Godbrothers and friends. If someone left, a couple of our Godbrothers left, and would lament and check about them and try to find out what they were doing. He was always concerned for other's welfare.

He was a connoisseur of food. He said Srila Prabhupada trained him how to eat in India. He could give reports to the cook and tell them what exactly what went wrong.

In Auckland once, during Srila Prabhupada's tirobhava there was a big feast. Pizza was his favourite. He ate it, and he was so Krsna conscious and asked if pizza was available in the spiritual world. The devotees were discussing and had so many opinions. Then he said to check Brhad-Bhagavatmrta to see when Krsna eats with the cowherd boys to see if pizza is there!

He was often misunderstood though he was actually loving. Never saw himself as superior. He would check with devotees about his activities, and we'd reassure him: "You can defeat the scholars; you should study." Now who will carry that flag? His Godbrothers. We should have faith in one another and love each other. By sharing and being kind, we will make progress because we have the qualities of devotees.

I would like to say a few words also about Mother Vrndavanesvari. She loved my Guru Maharaja and attended all his classes and always asked questions. She was a good book distributor. She had faith in her Guru Maharaja. Krsna took her and my Guru Maharaja away quickly so that we can learn from them what to do and how to do it. Then we get the benefits of the ISKCON movement.

Bhakti Bhrnga Govinda Maharaja...

I want to speak briefly before singing for his pleasure. I met him in the 70's in India, but really my relationship started only in the mid-80's. I met him after one of our Godbrothers left Krsna consciousness. A feeling of frustration or despair was there in my life. Tamal Krishna Goswami came on the horizon. Many were saying "No, no, don't go near him. It'll only be problematic." At first it was a bit, then I realized how sweet and loving he was. Other side was there, strict, demanding, sharp, but he was a man who was looking so much for affection. He simply wanted loving exchanges, it touched my heart.

I was with him in 1987. It was a winter morning in his garden. I said to him: "You are so fortunate to be with Srila Prabhupada so much. Tell me the best memories you have. He smiled and said "Yes, in the early days in LA people were complaining about me controlling them too much. Srila Prabhupada called me and then told how Krsna is in Goloka, and from Him expand so many universes, then there are so many planets; one is the earth, then so many continents; one is North America, then so many cities, like Los Angeles which had millions of people. Of all these people, there is one street, one house, one room, and one Tamal Krishna who thinks himself the supreme controller." Maharaja smiled and said "Srila Prabhupada understood where I was at."

He told me another one about fighting for the Juhu land. All of you know this about Mr. Nair, etc. Then he said that Srila Prabhupada and him were in South India and they heard that the deed was signed by Nair. So Srila Prabhupada sent him back to Bombay to get the deed. We had won. But Nair bribed the lawyer and the lawyer convinced Tamal Krishna Goswami that the deed was no good and should be cancelled. He did so. And then he told this to Srila Prabhupada on the phone. Srila Prabhupada was upset. "What! No, The deed has not been cancelled." And Srila Prabhupada hung up.

Then Srila Prabhupada came to Bombay. He was dealing with the top members of society for darshan. He would always call for Tamal Krishna Goswami in the darshan and Srila Prabhupada would introduce him as my American disciple – he is a great fool." Tamal Krishna Goswami was so pleased with this and said "Srila Prabhupada knew how to deal with me like no-one else could."

Once in 1989 we were in Vrndavana. It was 2:00 am. Someone came to my room knocking on the window. I was surprised. It was Maharaja's servant: "Tamal Krishna Goswami has to see you now!" "Now, it's 2am!" But I obediently got ready and went to him. He was in a state. He could get worked up, and he said "Prabhu, I need association of my Godbrothers badly. Visnujana has left. I want it, I need it to protect me. Now I'm in China you don't know what they are like there. He then spoke about Jayapataka Swami. Jayapataka Swami is so pious. Just looking at him you can see his piety. He had so much of Srila Prabhupada's association. Just see his service! If only I could get his sanga! And Bhakti Caru Swami is so wonderful! Always so busy! And Sivarama Swami, he such a wonderful Vaisnava, so pious! So please give me your association."

I was overwhelmed and said, "But they are all so pious, not me!" "No, I know you are not pious, but still I want your association!" (laughter)

So many said he was like a blazing chutney, but sugar-candy sweet also. It is a great loss for me, like a brother. I was thinking in our family of ISKCON there are so many brothers and sisters. Even our material brothers might please or displease us but still we must love them. I have this memory of him, that all of ISKCON at this time, whether you have displeasing or pleasing memories, now simply remember him with love.

And he liked my singing so we'll sing Hare Krishna for his pleasure and Srila Prabhupada and Radha Madhava. (Hare Krishna kirtana for 15 minutes.)

Jayadvaita Swami...

He would appreciate me saying this, and I can say with confidence that there is no other devotee in our society so admired and loved by so many devotees who so often disagreed with him. I did so many aparadhas against him and still he kept sweet affection for me, and me to him likewise.

Message from Bhavananda Das ...
(Read out by Sivarama Swami)

Tamal Krishna Goswami is my dearest and first friend in ISKCON. I will suffer his loss for the rest of my life. First I lost my spiritual master and now I lost my best friend.

Your servant, Bhavananda Das

HH Indradyumna Swami...

Dear Tamal Krsna Goswami,
Please accept my most humble obeisances. All glories to Srila Prabhupada.

Today I am writing you a posthumous letter, just as our spiritual master, Srila Prabhupada, did in the assembly of his disciples in Seattle when his Godbrother, Bhakti Prajna Kesvava Maharaja, passed away in 1968.

At that time Srila Prabhupada wrote:

"Be it resolved that we the undersigned members and devotees of the International Society for Krishna Consciousness in a condolence meeting, express our profound bereavement on hearing of the passing of Kesava Goswami Maharaja, our sannyasa guru."

Goswami Maharaja, this evening a number of your Godbrothers, disciples, friends and well-wishers are also expressing our profound bereavement that, by the mysterious plan of the Lord, you have suddenly been taken from our vision. We are still in a state of shock as to how we have become bereft of one of ISKCON's great Sankirtan generals. Each of us feels the loss in a different way: your Godbrothers miss your sweet Krsna conscious association, your disciples miss your loving care, the congregation miss your awe-inspiring leadership, and even newcomers who may be present tonight will miss the chance of ever meeting you, who could charm the hearts of so many conditioned souls by your preaching and bestow upon them the priceless gift of devotional service to Srila Prabhupada and Lord Krsna.

As for myself, Goswami Maharaja, with your departure I have lost a dear most friend who had my real interest at heart and who extended himself to me on numerous occasions. Our association goes back to the mid-1970s, when each year you, Bhagavan das and myself would go on a spiritual retreat to the sacred abode of Hrisikesh in the Himalayas. There we would read and chant, swim in the Ganga and have kirtans, just the three of us, in the spiritual atmosphere of that sacred abode. It was during those retreats that I imbibed from you (and you alone) a great zeal for the missionary activities of Krsna consciousness, for you would always preach to me the glories of the holy names, book distribution and the making of devotees.

But what amazed me the most was your brilliant plans and strategies for organizing these activities. Recognizing these abilities early in your devotional career, Srila Prabhupada entrusted you with the most responsible services, such as being part of the first Governing Body Commission, acquiring and securing the land for our Mayapur project in India, and heading up book distribution in America. Srila Prabhupada's supreme love and trust in you was demonstrated by his making you his personal secretary - a service you executed faithfully for so many years up to the very moment of his departure.

As a result of that service, you had an intimate look into the life of a pure devotee, something which you have shared freely with us all these years. You were part of a rare breed of devotees, Goswami Maharaja - devotees who had intimate association of his Divine Grace and understood his mood and the particular way he did things for Krsna. No doubt, you earned the most prestigious title any ISKCON devotee could earn, for you were in every way a "Prabhupada Man."

As a new devotee, when I first met you I was in awe and reverence - perhaps fear is a better word. Like a commander leading the troops in Lord Caitanya's army, you instilled such sentiments in your followers in order to push forward the Sankirtan movement, as if in military fashion.

Unfortunately, some devotees saw you only in that light. They didn't have the good fortune to know your soft heart, your love for the devotees, your thirst for associating with your Godbrothers, and your eagerness to attain Vrndavana and the loving mood of the Vrajabasis. You once showed your kinder face to me, when I approached you with the desire to take sannyasa in 1978 at the Gaura-Purnima Festival in India. Being an itinerant preacher since the day I joined the Krsna consciousness movement, I had a strong desire to leave householder life and enter the

renounced order. When I revealed my desire to my GBC representative, he replied, "Go and ask Tamal Krsna Maharaja. If he agrees, then I'll accept your request to take sannyasa."

Petrified, I approached you on top of the Long Building in Mayapur. I revealed my desire and awaited a grueling interview regarding my plans and motivations. Instead, you sat down with me, and after a few questions about my determination to preach, you gave me much advice on how to practice the life of a sannyasi. I continue to follow those guidelines to this day.

In 1980, when we were together at the Los Angeles Ratha-yatra, you pulled me to one side and aid,

"Indra, let's form a team - me and you. We'll travel all over America, all over the world, just like I did with Visnujana Maharaja. You'll lead kirtan and I'll speak. We'll make devotees everywhere." Goswami Maharaja, how much I lament now that I didn't take up your offer. I also lament not accepting your many invitations to visit you in Dallas, in Vrndavana, in Cambridge and in Oxford through the years. Of all my Godbrothers, I see you most appreciated and understood the value and need for associating with devotees, especially with Godbrothers. I am distraught that in this lifetime I won't have your association again. I won't hear your clear, logical and dynamic lectures. Goswami Maharaja, among all the devotees, you were my favorite Srimad-Bhagavatam speaker. What nectar you could have given us during the next twenty years. It's hard for me to understand why Krsna took you now, at this particular moment. You had so much to offer. You had so much association with Srila Prabhupada, so much experience in Krsna consciousness, so many ideas for spreading the movement. And you were on the verge of a new and promising career in devotional service. It can mean only that Krsna has a greater plan for you. I'm somewhat jealous of those who will soon be serving alongside you. With you, Krsna consciousness was full of life - spiritual life. It's not that you didn't have your problems to deal with, Goswami Maharaja. I remember our long talks in Cambridge last year. You indicated your dissatisfaction with the ways things were developing in some parts of our movement, you had your opponents, and you had personal concerns over your health. But throughout it all, you remained chaste and loyal to Srila Prabhupada and his ISKCON movement. You were a pillar of strength for others, you were the best of spiritual fathers to your disciples, you were the best of friends to those who chose to love you, you were the inspiration for masses of devotees, and you displayed real compassion to the fallen conditioned souls by undergoing so many austerities in the pioneer days of Krsna consciousness and in the recent spreading of our movement in China.

In a number of fields you were the first, although I saw that you always cultivated the spirit of servant. And now, in typical fashion, but in an unlikely way, you are the first of the initiating spiritual masters to be placed in samadhi at Mayapur. Your departure and its circumstances were tragic. But death is always tragic - and even more so when a devotee leaves this world. With the departure of any devotee, especially one of your caliber, the world becomes a little less fortunate. Devotees are the ONLY good fortune in Kali-yuga - and they are few and far between. Thus my lamentation is all the more deeper today, for my beloved disciple, Vrindavanesvari dasi, also passed away in the same accident as you. We mourn your demise, Goswami Maharaja. I know my life won't be the same. Sankirtan, our primary activity, is based on the principle of teamwork. When one of the primary individuals is removed from the equation, we lose a little of our endurance, a little of the wind is knocked out of us. I'll miss you, Goswami Maharaja. I'll miss your presence on the battlefield of preaching, and I'll miss our discussions in Vrndavana on Vraja-bhakti. Who will I turn to now with my questions on how to love Krsna? But as tragic as your departure was, it was also glorious. You gave up your body in the holy Mayapur Dhama near Phuliya, the very village that Haridas Thakur chanted 300,000 names of the Lord a day. You departed on the Disappearance Day of Jagannath das Babaji and Rasikananda prabhu.

Your samadhi ceremony was attended by all our movement's GBC men, many sannyasis, most of the temple presidents, and masses of devotees. Your samadhi ceremony was befitting a devotee of your stature, a devotee of your accomplishments - a devotee loved by many, many Godbrothers, disciples, friends, and scholars, as well as common people. We were together when my disciple Vraja Lila passed away in Vrndavana in 1997. At that time, you said that following her departure she would then be in a transcendental position to bless us all. Goswami Maharaja, you are also now in a transcendental position to bless me. Whether you are back home, back to Godhead, or are again the personal secretary of our beloved spiritual master, Srila Prabhupada, as he continues to establish Lord Caitanya's missionary movement in this material world, you are blessed, no doubt. So please continue to remember and think fondly of me, as always. And Goswami Maharaja, the next time you ask me to be your partner, to be a team, I won't be so foolish as to refuse. I'll be happy to lead the kirtans . . . and you can give the classes. By your mercy I'm a sannyasi, and ready to follow you anywhere.

Your servant, Indradyumna Swami

Hridayananda Maharaja (en espanol)...

Querido Brahma Tirtha Prabhu,

Todas las Glorias a Srila Prabhupada,

Aqui está mi declaración sobre Tamal Krishna Goswami. Por favor envielo al His Divine Grace istaghosti. Debido a que Su Santidad Tamal Krishna Goswami fue tan grande sirviente de Srila Prabhupada, su partida es una poderosa enseṣanza de Conciencia de Krishna que nos coloca cerca de Srila Prabhupada y del Seṣor Krishna. Oro para que todos honremos a Tamal Krishna Goswami mediante la asimilación profunda de las muchas preciadas lecciones que el nos ha dado a lo largo de su vida, sus enseṣanzas, su escritura e incluso su gloriosa desaparición en el mas auspicioso tiempo y lugar, en presencia de muchos excelsos vaishnavas. Srila Prabhupada siempre lo llamará para rendir poderosos y únicos servicios, y como todos sabemos sin lugar a dudas Srila Prabhupada ha llamado nuevamente a su mano derecha Tamala Krishna Goswami, para otro servicio, para hacer nuevamente lo que solo īl puede hacer.

Uno no puede sino observar a lo largo del mundo entero la masiva espontánea y sentida efusión de amor, honra y devoción por Tamal Krishna Goswami. Verdaderamente, la intensidad de la aflicción, el shock y la amorosa admiración es secundaria solo ante la demostrada hacia el propio Srila Prabhupada. Anoche, en un íntimo programa hogareșo en Minnesota, USA hablī extensamente sobre la larga lista de distinguidos e inimitables logros de Goswami Maharaja en el servicio al Seșor Krishna. No repetirī esa lista aqui, sino mas bien concluirī con una cordial observación personal: Continuando incluso con mas de su glorioso servicio devocional el gran vaishnava Tamal Krishna Goswami ha dado un gigantesco paso hacia la realización de aún otro de sus apreciados propósitos: el restablecimiento de la profunda generosa y amorosa cultura vaishnava en ISKCON. La enorme ola de aprecio y afección por īl, la cual ya inunda el mundo de ISKCON y que está creciendo diariamente, ya ha comenzado a arrastrar așos de cinismo y escepticismo acumulados. La fe está reemplazando a la duda. La generosidad está reemplazando a la renuencia. El amor está reemplazando el rencor. Los devotos están declarando libremente al mundo que un gran vaishnava ha partido y al así hacerlo, ellos personal y profundamente reconocen y agradecen que el querido discípulo de Srila Prabhupada, Tamal Krishna Goswami fue verdaderamente un gran vaishnava. Todos nosotros en nuestro pesar exclamamos que īste fue un excelso sirviente de Srila Prabhupada, una gran alma que jugó una enorme parte en la transformación del mundo. Los devotos en todas partes están viendo que cada entidad viviente que se ve beneficiada por el Movimiento de Srila Prabhupada tiene una eterna deuda para con Su Santidad Tamala Krishna Goswami quien hizo mas de lo que las palabras puedan contar para servir a la misión de su eterno maestro espiritual Srila Prabhupada. Regocijemonos en nuestro conocimiento cierto de que Tamala Krishna Goswami regresará ahora rápidamente al servicio personal de su eterno maestro espiritual, un servicio que īl valora por sobre todas las cosas.

de tu hermano menor y anhelante sirviente,
Hridayananda das Goswami

Bhakti Vikasa Swami...

Krsna has yet again shown that He is inconceivable. No one can be kinder than Krsna, and Krsna is particularly the well-wisher and protector of His devotees. Yet Krsna's arrangements are unpredictable and sometimes why and what He does is unimaginable and apparently even horrible.

Just as, yesterday Krsna decided to take Tamal Krsna Goswami to Him. Dozens of deaths occur on the Indian roads every day, but this was not just another statistic. Krsna personally cares for His devotees, and this event could not have taken place without His direct sanction. Why should Krsna take Tamal Krsna Maharaja so suddenly, prematurely, with his service unfinished, and in such a cruel manner? Krsna knows.

Krsna declares: kaunteya pratijanihi na me bhakta pranasyati, and it is the devotee's faith that no matter how nasty and intolerable or even absurd Krsna's arrangements may seem to be, they are always for the ultimate welfare of His devotees.

Again and again we ask ourselves, "Is this real? Has it really happened?" and again and again the events of yesterday reappear in our minds to convince us that they are indeed true. Yesterday afternoon as I intently looked in the face of Tamal Krsna Maharaja, a face as strong and firm as

ever yet now peaceful as maybe never before previously, I realized that what we had heard that morning and which by the behavior of all present seemed must be true, but about which we were reserving a hope that it might nevertheless be some fantastic misunderstanding, was indeed a fact.

Hundreds of devotees had congregated in Mayapura, the very abode of happiness, for a blissful festival of chanting and dancing. Yesterday, however, there was another kind of festival. The chanting and dancing went on, yet on hundreds of faces accustomed to smile, we saw only sadness.

But happiness was not completely absent. When Sridhar Maharaja announced that Tamal Krsna Maharaja had gone to Krsna, a chorus of spontaneous wails went up from the womenfolk. Yet simultaneously there was a single joyful "Haribol!" Narasimha Maharaja, who had all these years so selflessly assisted Tamal Krsna Maharaja, in grief buried his head in Sridhar Maharaja's shoulder, yet he also joined the joyful chanting and dancing that ensued shortly thereafter; for the passing of a Vaisnava is a time of celebration as well as lamentation. Madhava was still smiling, as was His Radha and Her sakhis. And so surely was Tamal Krsna Maharaja, smiling down at us from his eternal abode in the pastimes of Sri Sri Radha Madhava.

He reasons ill who tells that Vaisnavas die
when thou art living still in sound
A Vaisnava dies to live
And living tries to spread the holy name around.

Tamal Krsna Maharaja is still present among us in many ways, not least in the form of his disciples, some of whom are clearly very advanced souls. We request Maharaja's disciples to continue to spread the fame of your guru-maharaja by maintaining an exemplary standard that he-and we-can be proud of. Always pushing you to come to the highest standard, your guru-maharaja tested you in many ways, sometimes almost unbearably. But now is your greatest test, since the love of disciples for their guru is not known so much by how they serve him in his presence, as by how they continue to do so in his absence.

I'll also take this opportunity to thank all devotees present and not present for the wonderful services they have performed over all these years, and to beg forgiveness for all my offenses to them. We never know when Krsna will take His devotee to His abode, so it's better to say the most important things while we can.

Sri Sri Radha Madhava ki jaya.

Their eternal servant Srila Tamala Krishna Goswami Maharaja ki jay.

HH Bhakti Brnga Govinda Swami...

(a recounting of Tamal Krishna Goswami's passing)

Dear Vaisnava Community,

Please accept my humble obeisances. All glories to Srila Prabhupada.

Tamal Krishna Goswami joined us in kirtan every evening prior to his departure. For many nights the kirtan had been conducted in his quarters. No invitation was required. When the doors opened the room quickly filled to capacity with devotees, young and old, eager to enter into the nectarean chanting of the Lord's holy names.

This was really the spiritual highlight of each day. It was the event that gave meaning to being in Mayapur. We all sat together, with one of our most elder brothers, a loving family of devotees, singing the names of Sri Radha and Sri Krishna with deep feeling.

On the last few evenings of Tamal Krishna Goswami's presence the kirtan shifted to the Panca Tattva Temple. This was done due to the increasing size of the crowd. On his last evening in Mayapur he came from the main pandal program. Having finished speaking he joined the kirtan. After an hour of kirtan he reached over, held my hand, and thanked me for being in kirtan with him. Then he told me, "tomorrow I will be leaving." I asked him where he was going and he said , " back to home ... and after a pause he said ... back to the UK."

I thanked him for his association and told him I would try to see him off the next morning. Tamal Krishna Goswami left for Kolkatta at 4:15. He was accompanied by Vrindavanesvari and Kalasambara of Auckland, New Zealand and his disciple Aghavit. I sang mangala arati that morning for the pleasure of Radha Madhava. During the Tulasi puja I sat next to Sivaram Swami to begin chanting my Japa. I looked up and saw Tamal Krishna Maharaja's cook, Gopal Raja, quickly walking by. I reached out and took his hand and asked him if Maharaja had departed on time. Gopal Raja responded by saying a phone call had just come that there had been a serious accident and Tamal Krishna Maharaja was unconscious. This was around 5:15 AM. So it appears that the accident occurred during Brahma Muhurta at the conclusion of Mangala Arati.

I related this news to Sivaram Maharaja. We both jumped up and Sivaram Maharaja ran to Jayapataka Swami. Immediately we went outside and began to arrange vehicles. The morning festival announcements had begun. I returned to the temple, took the microphone, and informed the devotees of the tragic news we had just received. I requested the devotees to silently pray to the feet of Lord Narasingha and Radha Madhava for the safety of Goswami Maharaja and the members of his party. After a minute of silent prayer I ran from the temple room.

Vehicles were organized. In our car there were Jayapataka Swami, Sivaram Swami, Niranjana Swami, Jayadvaita Swami, myself and a few Bengali devotees. We immediately left for the site. The place of the accident is a village on the main highway called Phulia. This is the holy site where Namacarya Haridasa Thakur lived in a crocodile hole on the banks of the Ganga. Here he chanted three hundred thousand holy names a day, was beaten in twenty two market places, and was tempted by Mayadevi personified and ultimately initiated her.

We came off the Santipur bypass and proceeded for some time. Two cars from the opposite direction stopped us to inform that there had been a terrible accident on the highway. As we approached we saw the car sitting upright, but sideways, on the highway. All of the windows were smashed and the left top side of the vehicle was somewhat collapsed. There was a large crowd at the site. As we reached the spot we found devotees in hysteria. They informed that the all of the wounded had been taken to Ranaghat Hospital. They also informed that Goswami Maharaja was unconscious.

We reached the hospital we again found hysterical grieving vaisnavas. We were taken immediately to the room where Goswami Maharaja's body was laying. At one glance I could see that He had left his body. I mentioned this to Niranjana Swami and in shock we offered our obeisances to Maharaja. We touched our heads to the feet of that great servant of Srila Prabhupada and prayed that Prabhupada's and Krishna's mercy be fully with him. From the report of Kalasamvara prabhu the accident took place on a very straight stretch of road. There were no obstructions on the highway and no traffic from the opposite direction.

It appears that the driver of Tamal Krishna Goswami's Tata Sumo fell asleep at the wheel. At high speed the Sumo sideswiped a very large tree on the left side of the road. The vehicle lost balance and began rolling. The front left side of the cabin caved in. Goswami Maharaja was sitting in the front left passenger seat with his seat belt fastened. Vrindavanesvari was sitting directly behind him. These two took the full brunt of the high speed collision and roll.

Kalasambara was able to free himself from the car. He first tried to remove Goswami Maharaja but soon realized that his body was lifeless. Kalasamvara Prabhu is quite certain that Goswami Maharaja had left His body immediately upon impact. He then removed Vrindavanesvari and Aghavit from the car and placed all the injured into the second car that had been following them. They proceeded to the Ranaghat Hospital. Kalasamvara's perception was confirmed at the hospital. Goswami Maharaja had immediately given up his body during the accident. Vrindavanesvari suffered severe head damage and was given minimal chance of survival. Although an arrangement had been made to transfer her to Kolkatta, she gave up her body minutes later on the floor of the women's ward. When she passed away Sivaram Swami and Niranjana Swami were softly singing the Hare Krishna Maha Mantra.

Jayapataka Swami diligently walked through the situation with the police investigators and doctors. He was trying very tactfully to get immediate release of the bodies but it was not allowed. According to Indian Law all accidental deaths require a postmortem. We tried to explain that Goswami Maharaja was an acarya. There was an agreement that the postmortem doctor would make the smallest minimal incision on the bodies of Goswami Maharaja and Vrindavanesvari. Around 11 AM we carried his body to the morgue. After 12 PM the postmortem doctor came and performed his work. Jayapataka Maharaja succeeded in having all papers signed by 3 PM. We placed the bodies of Goswami Maharaja and Vrindavanesvari inside of the sankirtan bus and were ready to leave for Mayapur.

Then another problem arose. There were at least 200 local people that refused to allow our bus to roll until they had darshan of Maharaja's face. We said that they should take darshan of his feet but they insisted that as he was a mahatma they had to see his face. We were hesitant, but the crowd became unruly. As soon as we showed them Maharaja's face they all began to chant Maha Mantra and offer pranam. Then they allowed us to leave. Even though Santipur is traditionally a place of Vaisnava offenders, as the bus passed through the streets, the people chanted Hare Krishna and showed respect by folding their palms.

We reached Mayapur around 4:30 PM. There was an ocean of grieving vaisnavas waiting at the gate. The bus moved slowly down the main drive to the main guest house building and turned right.

Kirtan was being led by Lokanath Maharaja. The bodies were removed from the bus and taken to different rooms at the rear of the guesthouse. There they were prepared for the respective funeral ceremonies. The ladies who were preparing the body of HG Vrindavanesvari noted that all of her limbs were still soft and supple. Only her right hand, which was formed in the position of a person holding japa beads, was erect and immovable.

After cleansing her remains she was carried to the shores of Mother Ganga and cremated. It was the actual birthday of Vrindavanesvari. She wanted the special privilege and birthday gift of riding in the car to Kolkatta with Goswami Maharaja. But She actually received the priceless gift of riding back to Godhead with her beloved friend and siksa guru Tamal Krishna Goswami.

Goswami Maharaja's body was bathed, massaged in ghee, mantras were written in sandal paste upon his body, he was dressed in new cloth, and was profusely covered with garlands. His body was then placed upon a stretcher and carried on procession around the Deities. For nearly forty five minutes His remains rested on the platform in front of Sri Sri Radha Madhava for final darshan. The assembled vaisnavas filed by and had their final darshan of Goswami Maharaja. During this darshan the kirtan was sweetly sung by Niranjana Swami.

Then the procession left for the samadhi of Srila Prabhupada. His remains were shown to Prabhupada in the samadhi and there was circumambulation of Srila Prabhupada. The procession left the samadhi and proceeded to the selected site of Maharaja's samadhi. He was slowly lowered into the samadhi pit. Puja was conducted and his feet were washed. He was offered bhoga and arati was performed. Flowers were then tossed upon his remains and some were collected to be used in the Puspasamadhi that will be erected at ISKCON Bhaktivedanta Ashrama in Govardhan. The body of HH Tamal Krishna Goswami was first covered with salt and then earth. The site of Goswami Maharaja's samadhi is on the left side of the parikrama path around Srila Prabhupada's samadhi. It is just near the point where the path turns left to proceed to the grhasta living area. It is an area which has been designated in the Mayapur City master plan for samadhis.

On Saturday there was a remembrance ceremony for HH Tamal Krishna Goswami Maharaja and HG Vrindavanesvari Devi Dasi. The ceremony was overseen by HH Sivaram Maharaja. Many senior devotees spoke of their deep appreciation, affection, and love for both of these unique and wonderful souls. Tamal Krishna Maharaja was recognized as a dedicated servant of Srila Prabhupada. The quantity, quality and varieties of services he performed for Srila Prabhupada's pleasure was amazing. Many devotees acknowledged that he was a strict disciplinarian, sharp, and demanding. But all who spoke shared a vision of a Goswami Maharaja who was not simply the stereotypical demanding controller: But of a gentle and extremely soft hearted Vaisnava who relished sharing love with all.

A charming and eloquent person that had an enormous capacity to give shelter, guidance, care, instruction, and affectionate love to many many people. A master of wit and cleverness. A connoisseur of fine prasadam. An enigma. A misunderstood person. A person who was like chutney ... unbearably hot and irresistibly sweet simultaneously. A person who Prabhupada could always depend upon. A person who could rise to overcome any challenge for the service of Srila Prabhupada. A person who Prabhupada would always call to help in times of need. A person who served Prabhupada with deep unflinching love during the final days of His Divine Grace. A person who was a general in Srila Prabhupada's Sankirtan Army. A person who courted controversy. A person who made mistakes but never gave up his determination to serve the feet of Srila Prabhupada. A person who inspired thousands of devotees with his wonderful classes. A self denigrating and humble person. A person who peace craftily eluded. As Srila Prabhupada said, a man desperate to do anything for the service of Guru and Gauranga.

Her Grace Vrindavanesvari was remembered as a great sankirtan devotee, a massive collector who was always short of funds because she never kept for herself, a caring wife, a wonderful mother, an amazingly talented cook, a kind person who never ran short on big smiles, and most profoundly, a lover of the holy names of the Lord. She could chant japa and kirtan endlessly with great taste and devotion.

After many hours of loving remembrances there was the pushpanjali ceremony followed by arati to the photo of Goswami Maharaja. The kirtan was led by one of his dearest and closest friends Kesava Bharati prabhu. After which there was a wonderful feast offered to Radha Madhava in remembrance of HH Tamal Krishna Goswami Maharaja. All of the disciples of Srila Prabhupada honored prasadam on the veranda where the GBC have prasad. At the head of the line of all of the vaisnavas was a table of Radha Madhava's Mahaprasadam and seated in front of that table was an asana with the picture of Goswami Maharaja. After relishing the feast we all partook of his remnants. The passing of His Divine Grace Tamal Krishna Goswami Maharaja and Vrindavanesvari Mataji has filled our hearts with devastation and sadness. For many of us they were close friends, a brother, a sister, a sincere well-wisher.

Their departure marks a great loss for our International Society for Krishna Consciousness. Such wonderful and glorious vaisnavas possessed with the ceaseless determination to preach are so rare and hard to find. But we are happy for them and are perfectly assured that they have both

gone back home to serve in the realm beyond tears.

We are especially happy that Goswami Maharaja has now captured the peace that so long eluded him by again attaining the association of His Beloved Spiritual Master Srila Prabhupada and Their Divine Lordship Sri Sri Radha Shyamsundar.

Srila Tamal Krishna Goswami Maharaja Ki Jai !! Srimati Vrindavanesvari devi dasi Ki Jai !!

Srila Prabhupada Ki Jai !! Giriraja Govardhan Ki Jai !! Gaura Premanande !! Hari Bol !! The Pushpa Samadhi ceremony of His Divine Grace Tamal Krishna Goswami Maharaja will be conducted at ISKCON Bhaktivedanta Ashrama, Govardhan, on March 22, 2001.

With affectionate regards,

Bhakti Brnga Govinda Swami

ANECDOTES FROM Tamal Krishna Goswami...

The devotees invited me to a darshan where I heard Prabhupada beautifully sing the Chintamani prayers. Afterwards he asked if anyone had any questions and I raised my hand. At that time America was at war with Vietnam and at our age the draft board was a problem. I was very concerned about whether or not I would be drafted, and so I asked Prabhupada to describe what the spiritual world was like. He looked at me and said, In the spiritual world there are no draft boards. Then he told a story. He said, There was once a Christian minister who was preaching in England to coal miners. He said that the hell that awaited someone if they didn't accept the shelter of Jesus was a terrible place, dark, dank, cold, and wet. He said, No one would want to go there, but all of the coal miners were thinking, Well, if that's hell, where are we? We're already in hell. It doesn't sound very fearful to us. That's where we live now, we're coal miners. The minister was trying to think of a way to convince them to worship Jesus and finally he said, In hell, there are no newspapers and there is no tea. Then they all said, Oh, then we must worship Jesus. Prabhupada said, So in the spiritual world, there are no draft boards. Is that all right? I said, Yes, and everybody said, Jai.

The first time Prabhupada saw me with a shaved head he said, Ah, now you are an ideal brahmachari. He was pleased that I had shaved my head because although I had been keeping my hair short, I wouldn't shave up. I had joined with Vishnujana and he had shaved up, but I hadn't. When I finally did, Prabhupada appreciated it. On the first walk I went on I asked Prabhupada, How many pure devotees are there on the planet? Srila Prabhupada asked, How many devotees are there in ISKCON now? That is how many pure devotees there are.

We made about twelve dollars the first day. I went back to the temple and said, Gargamuni, we did twelve dollars. He said, Wow. I'm gonna give up my shop. This is big, this has huge potential. The next day I decided to take Back to Godhead Magazines with us, and when people give a donation I give them a Back to Godhead. By the end of five days the collections had gone up to forty dollars. I wrote Prabhupada day by day how it was increasing. Prabhupada wrote me, Don't worry so much about money. If Krishna wants to, He can give you the whole USA. The question is what will you do with it? Do you know what to do with it? It was a sobering letter.

In the early days I was the temple commander in the La Cienega temple in Los Angeles. Prabhupada called me one day and asked me to get the Bhagavatam. He had his original Bhagavatam with the spiritual sky on the cover. He said, Do you see this spiritual sky? It's very big. You cannot fathom how big this is. Three-quarters of Krishna's creation is the spiritual sky and one-quarter is the material creation. That material creation has innumerable universes. One universe is so big the scientists can't measure it. We're on one planet in one of those universes out of innumerable universes, which constitute one-quarter of the creation. This one planet, earth is one of the smaller planets in this universe. On this planet there are seven continents, and on one of the continents, North America, there is a great city called Los Angeles. In that Los Angeles city, there's a long boulevard called La Cienega. On that La Cienega Boulevard, there is one church building that is now a Hare Krishna Temple. In that one Hare Krishna Temple, there is one Tamal Krishna, and he thinks that he is very important. (Laughs) I felt so small.

Before the operation began, they gave me an anesthetic and said, Count from ten, down. I got to about seven and that was it. I was meditating on Radha Rasabihari in the aratik and then I had a very good dream. In my dream Srila Prabhupada had been called by the previous acharyas to make a report on his preaching mission on this planet. The previous acharyas asked Prabhupada, What is your report? Prabhupada said that he had studied the people of this planet and he had found that they had no capacity for any type of austerity. Nor were they very capable of studying, nor were they very pious. He said the only thing that they were able to do was, somehow take shelter at my feet.

After the operation they wheeled me to my assigned room. Prabhupada was sitting there. He said, I came here as fast as I could. I wanted to stop the operation because I think you should have had this operation in America, but anyway it is done now. He had come all the way from Juhu in a jeep in the middle of the rush hour to try to stop the operation. I told Prabhupada about the dream. Prabhupada listened very intently and said, Actually, this is so. ("Memories" of HH Tamal Krishna Goswami (Tapes 10, 11, 16 & 29; itv@flash.net)

CHAPTER 3: ISKCON

HOW ALL GENERATIONS CAN STAY WITH SRILA PRABHUPADA

by His Holiness Satsvarupa dasa Goswami

Service to Srila Prabhupada Across the Generations

Writing the last chapter of the Srila Prabhupada-lilamrita was an intense experience for me. Prabhupada was teaching "the final lesson," and I relived the day-by-day remembrances of being with Srila Prabhupada and serving in his ISKCON movement in the final days leading up to his disappearance. Those days were like a drama unfolding. Would Prabhupada stay with us? What would we do without him? And again I felt the grief at his departure. I was also reminded that Prabhupada's last days were filled with the preaching spirit as he encouraged his disciples to continue his work. He exemplified calm and tolerance in the face of great pain, and fearlessness in the face of death. He allowed us the intimacy of chanting soft kirtanas in his room and reading to him from Srimad-Bhagavatam, Krishna book, and his other books.

Then it was again November 14, 1977 and Prabhupada departed at 7:30 p.m. In the Lilamrita I told briefly about Prabhupada's actual passing—how he left in perfect circumstances in Vrindavana after a life totally dedicated to Krishna, a life of incredibly potent achievements for Lord Caitanya's mission. I also told about how the news of Prabhupada's departure affected his disciples around the world.

Well, was that it? Biography finished? No. There was more. I had to tell about service in separation. Even though Prabhupada appeared to pass away from this world, he continues to live through his instructions. Service in separation, vipralambha-seva, is a high level of realization, something which the residents of Vrindavana feel in Krishna's absence. We too can feel a form of union in separation, even though we are not so advanced in spiritual realization, simply by meditating on Srila Prabhupada's presence and instructions.

He was gone but he was still very much present. This realization was not a pretension or a myth, nor was it sentimental or psychic phenomenon or mental telepathy—it was a completely substantive, palpable reality, a fact of life. Srila Prabhupada had given them personal service and now they would continue that service. Prabhupada was still present through his instruction and all the nectar of his direct association—all the nectar of Krishna consciousness that he had given and shared with them was still available.

Service in separation for Prabhupada's disciples was undoubtedly a fact. Otherwise, now that they were without his personal presence, how would they be able to sustain themselves in spiritual life? The fact that they could continue as before, increase their feelings of devotion, and increase their serving capacity, meant that Srila Prabhupada was still very much with them.

Now had I completed the biography? Again I found myself feeling that something more was needed. Therefore I wrote the Epilogue. I wanted readers to understand clearly that they too had a claim to a relationship with Srila Prabhupada. I expected that most of the readers would not be initiated disciples of His Divine Grace. In fact, I assumed that some of the readers might be encountering Srila Prabhupada for the first time in this book. Each of them could have a relationship with Prabhupada. It was their right. Otherwise, as touching as the biography of Srila Prabhupada might read, the reader would be left only with the idea that this was a story of one guru with his little band of disciples who tried to begin a worldwide movement. It had nothing to do with them and there was no way in which they could participate now since that guru had left this world. I wanted the reader to understand that Prabhupada was more than the guru of a particular generation; he was to be with us forever.

In describing how the followers of His Divine Grace A. C. Bhaktivedanta Swami Prabhupada continued to relish the nectar of serving him in separation, we are not speaking of only a small band of several thousand devotees whom he initiated during his lifetime. Srila Prabhupada was not only an acarya, but he was the founder-acarya of the Krishna consciousness movement, which is a dynamic spiritual reality.

We cannot limit Srila Prabhupada, therefore, by describing only the drama of his being the guru for one generation of followers. Srila Prabhupada is jagat-guru, the spiritual master of the entire world. He is a bona fide spiritual master, faithfully conveying the message of the disciplic succession from Lord Krishna, as he received it in parampara from his spiritual master. But more than that, he was empowered by Krishna to do what no other spiritual master has done. He is the founder-acarya for spreading Lord Caitanya's sankirtana worldwide in the midst of the age of Kali.

—SPL, Vol. 6, pp. 423–24

Such a personal relationship with the founder-acarya is possible even for persons not directly initiated by Srila Prabhupada. It was Srila Prabhupada who taught us to apply Krishna consciousness to the modern context. It was Srila Prabhupada who set the standards of sadhana and cleanliness, of purity and association. Whoever follows these basic practices and recognizes Srila Prabhupada as Krishna's direct representative is his follower.

In the Epilogue, I also pointed out that people could serve Krishna through their fields of endeavor—artists, philosophers, businessmen, and laborers could all become devotees. Srila Prabhupada placed few restrictions on his followers as to how they could serve. After all, he wanted Krishna consciousness to pervade the entire society and he felt that the Krishna conscious philosophy had jurisdiction over all subjects of learning and action. Why shouldn't anyone anywhere in the world feel that if he took up Prabhupada's instructions, he could become Srila Prabhupada's follower?

The Krishna conscious gifts Srila Prabhupada brought to the West are for everyone. Srila Prabhupada left us with a dynamic legacy in his books, through his devotees, in the development of his communities, and in his teachings of how to expertly apply Krishna consciousness of his communities, and in his teachings of how to expertly apply Krishna consciousness in every situation. If we simply use our intelligence to claim our relationship with Prabhupada by practicing Krishna consciousness in the mood in which he taught it, we will inherit the most wonderful relationship with Krishna's pure devotee, Srila Prabhupada.

That was the purpose of the Srila Prabhupada-lilamrita, and if anyone reads it and opens himself to the possibility of a deep relationship with Srila Prabhupada, he will not only become a Prabhupadanuga, but he will taste the sweetness of Prabhupada's association. This is true not only of persons who joined ISKCON during Prabhupada's physical presence but for those who joined after 1977.

Srila Prabhupada's Mission

A Prabhupadanuga has exclusive devotion to Prabhupada. He doesn't like to hear that Prabhupada is just one of many gurus teaching Gaudiya Vaishnavism and that there is little distinction between Prabhupada and any other Gaudiya teacher. A Prabhupadanuga recognizes Srila Prabhupada's special place among gurus of Gaudiya Vaishnavism.

What is that special place? To understand that, we have to understand some of the history of the Gaudiya Vaishnava mission. Lord Caitanya predicted, "In every town and village My name will be sung." For generations following the prophecy, Gaudiya Vaishnavas wondered what it could have meant. How could such a thing be achieved all over the world? Did Lord Caitanya refer only to every town and village in India?

Immediately after Lord Caitanya's departure, many brilliant acaryas appeared. Narottama dasa Thakura, Shyamananda Prabhu, Srinivasa Acarya, and Vishvanatha Cakravarti Thakura all appeared contemporaneously or in quick succession. Each of those acaryas propagated Lord Caitanya's mission in Gauda. Then after their disappearance, the Gaudiya mission became disturbed. There was a sudden proliferation of prakrita-sahajiya and other bogus sects—so many, in fact, that the average Bengali began to identify

Gaudiya Vaishnavism with a sex cult.

Some generations later, Srila Bhaktivinoda Thakura appeared and pioneered the reestablishment of the purity and solidity of Lord Caitanya's teachings, bringing the movement again to people's attention as the deep religious tradition that it is. He was assisted in his mission by his son, Srila Bhaktisiddhanta Sarasvati Thakura, whose attacks on Mayavadi philosophy and the growing secularism of India were powerful and effective.

Bhaktivinoda Thakura and his son were not only interested in defeating Mayavadis and other unbona fide religious expressions, however. Rather, the main thrust of their movement was to teach the yuga-dharma, the chanting of the holy name of Krishna. It is in this tradition that Srila Prabhupada appeared, and with this mission.

It is stated in the Caitanya-caritamrita, kali-kalera dharma—krishna-nama-sankirtana/ krishna-shakti vina nahe tara pravartana: "The fundamental religious system in the age of Kali is the chanting of the holy name of Krishna. Unless empowered by Krishna, one cannot propagate the sankirtana movement." (Cc., Antya 7.11) This verse underlines Srila Prabhupada's specialness: he was empowered to spread the sankirtana movement all over the world. It was he who fulfilled the prediction Lord Caitanya had made five hundred years earlier that His name would be spread to every town and village, not just of India, but of the world.

Srila Prabhupada's very human story of how he carried out this mission can capture our hearts. His courage and dedication inspire us to follow him, to love him, and to want to do great things on his behalf. He fought against great odds to carry out his spiritual master's legacy. He came to America at an advanced age with only a trunkful of books and the equivalent of eight dollars in his pocket, yet he was the wealthiest philanthropist. To accept his gift fully requires that we become exclusively his followers. As Prabhupada is no ordinary guru, so our following of him cannot be ordinary or diffused. Rather, it must be focused on his mood, his teachings, and his mission.

Guru-nishtha in ISKCON

Srila Prabhupada's mission is nondifferent from Srila Rupa Gosvami's mission. In his purport to Cc. Antya 1.117, Srila Prabhupada writes:

The special function of Srila Rupa Gosvami is to establish the feelings of Sri Caitanya Mahaprabhu. These feelings are His desires that His special mercy be spread throughout the world in this Kali-yuga. His desire is that all over the world, everyone, in every village and every town, know of Sri Caitanya Mahaprabhu and His sankirtana movement. These are the inner feelings of Sri Caitanya Mahaprabhu. Sri Rupa Gosvami committed to writing all these feelings of the Lord. Now again, by the mercy of Sri Caitanya Mahaprabhu, the same feeling are being spread all over the world by the servants of the Gosvamis, and devotees who are pure and simple will appreciate this attempt.

Srila Prabhupada also writes, "Advancement in Krishna consciousness depends on the attitude of the follower." (NOI, Introduction) All the shastras declare the necessity to accept all follow a bona fide spiritual master in parampara. "Following" implies accepting the spiritual master's particular mood and emphasis in his relationship with Krishna. Srila Prabhupada perfectly exemplified such following in his own relationship with Srila Bhaktisiddhanta Sarasvati Thakura, as was proven by his successful execution of the mission. Srila Prabhupada's own mood toward his Guru Maharaja was one of exclusive devotion and attention. We can follow that example.

Guru-nishtha is the most important point in spiritual life. In a lecture in Vrindavana (November 28, 1976), Srila Prabhupada states:

All you are young Westerners. You never study Vedanta, but you can surprise many so-called Vedantists how to understand Krishna. How it has become possible? Simply by your firm faith in your spiritual master and Krishna and chanting Hare Krishna. That's all. Yasya deve para bhaktir, yatha deve tatha gurau. This is the Vedic process. If we have got firm faith in guru and firm faith in Krishna—guru-krishna-krpaya paya bhakti-lata-bija—then you get the seedling of bhakti-lata.

There is a tendency now that time is passing to see things more objectively and to think that perhaps Srila Prabhupada wasn't so special. After all, he is just one more link in the parampara chain of innumerable gurus stemming from Krishna. Actually, ISKCON devotees are often accused by those outside ISKCON of being too exclusive in their devotion. Why should we claim a special place for Prabhupada or for any other guru for that matter? Even within ISKCON we can hear the advanced realizations of other devotees, or see them travel around the world, gain followers, write their own books. A follower of Prabhupada won't allow such minimization to creep into his faith. Srila Prabhupada accomplished something so extraordinary that any comparison to others becomes a minimization of his position.

This is the nature of an ISKCON devotee: he or she wants to develop love for Krishna by following strictly in Srila Prabhupada's footsteps and in the mood that he taught. It will be to the credit of Srila Prabhupada's disciples and succeeding generations of followers to continue with this fixed determination in their glorification of His Divine Grace A. C. Bhaktivedanta Swami Prabhupada. Such devotion is not fanatical. Prahlada Maharaja expressed a similar sentiment when describing his feelings toward his own spiritual master, Narada Muni:

My dear Lord, O Supreme Personality of Godhead, because of my association with material desires, one after another, I was gradually falling into a blind well full of snakes, following the general populace. But Your servant Narada Muni kindly accepted me as his disciple and instructed me how to achieve this transcendental position. Therefore, my first duty is to serve him. How could I leave his service? —Bhag. 7.9.28

I am sure that Srila Prabhupada would encourage this kind of exclusive devotion. He expressed such undiverted attention toward his own spiritual master, and he tried to protect ISKCON from the various outside influences that could disturb it or that would misunderstand his application of Krishna consciousness for Westerners. Such exclusive devotion is not the property of only those devotees who joined ISKCON before 1977; it is the property of all who wish to follow Prabhupada. We can cultivate that exclusive devotion to Prabhupada by hearing about his life, studying his teachings, praying to him, and rendering service to him according to his desires.

Srila Prabhupada Inspires Our Faith

Since devotion to Prabhupada necessarily includes following his instructions, it is useful to know what types of things please Srila Prabhupada. When he was confronted with the question, "Srila Prabhupada, how can we please you most," Prabhupada usually didn't offer a list of service or preaching engagements, but made the simple statement, "If you love Krishna." ("I have noted in your letter that you want to serve me. I only want that all you my disciples always think of Krishna and never forget Him for a moment. In this way you can conquer Krishna. He becomes so attracted by pure devotion that He gives Himself to His devotee. And if you get Krishna, then what you want more?")

Beyond that, however, Srila Prabhupada instructed us how to come to the stage of remembering Krishna at every moment, and that constituted the basis of his ISKCON movement. In order for us to engage in his movement, we needed to have faith. Srila Prabhupada created that faith in his followers, most of whom were hampered by the cynicism born of living in an age of atheism and sense enjoyment. We were able to have faith in Prabhupada because he was renounced, because he was saintly, because he was so honestly and obviously dedicated to God. There were no scandals in his life. He was able to create faith in the minds of those who had come to believe that God was dead, or, as the East Village Other put it, present only in LSD.

He also created faith by his strong lecturing in which he not only appealed to shastric authority, but to logic. "Let us come to reason," he would often say. The teachings—that we are eternal spirit soul, servants of God, and that real liberation is not to abandon our individuality but to fulfill our relationship with Krishna—he presented with strong yet simple arguments. We became convinced because the philosophy made sense; he made sense. He could answer all doubts, and he continues to do so in his books. Srila Prabhupada's whole life was gloriously supportive of his own faith in guru and Krishna. Because he embodied faith, he became worthy of our faith in a world where we had been cheated and disappointed again and again.

Gratitude and Obligation

When faith develops in a devotee, he or she naturally feels gratitude and obligation toward the spiritual master. This sense of gratitude and obligation helps Srila Prabhupada's followers to become the limbs by which he fulfills his own spiritual master's order. We all know that any Westerner who has heard the words "Hare Krishna" must have had some kind of contact with Srila Prabhupada or his followers, if only from a distance. It was Srila Prabhupada who made "Hare Krishna" a household word. Once when Srila Prabhupada was traveling with a stopover in Athens, Greece, he overheard some young man jokingly singing the Hare Krishna mantra. Prabhupada himself was amazed at how far the holy name had spread. Just to contemplate that—what we were before, what we have become, that we have learned to aspire for the highest goal of life—and that all this has become possible, not only for us but for hundreds of thousands of people by Srila Prabhupada's mercy can only increase our thankfulness.

Gratitude and obligation toward the guru are expressed through service. Following the spiritual master's orders is the real test of love and faith. When a follower is serious about a relationship with Srila Prabhupada, he or she will begin to receive knowledge from him. The spiritual master gives that knowledge freely, unofficially. When the follower begins to feel gratitude, that is an open acknowledgment of debt. Whether or not we acknowledge our debt openly, however, the debt is there. We have accepted something from the guru and we are obligated to reciprocate with him. That is the meaning of guru-dakshina.

What Did Srila Prabhupada Want?

Then what did Srila Prabhupada want? That we should love Krishna, yes, and that we should follow his instructions in order to attain that love. This is evidenced by the fact that as soon as people become serious, Srila Prabhupada introduced them to the traditional relationship of guru and disciple. He also introduced them to the four regulative principles: no meat-eating, no illicit sex, no intoxication, and no gambling. He established the standard that all initiated followers should chant sixteen rounds of the Hare Krishna mantra a day both to purify their hearts and to awaken their dormant love for Krishna. We cannot overemphasize Srila Prabhupada's importance in our lives as the giver of the holy name. That was his special contribution. Therefore, to follow this formula of avoiding sinful life and chanting and hearing about Krishna is the basic program Srila Prabhupada expected his followers to pursue. He also wanted us to cooperate with each other and to preach to the nondevotees.

Following the order of the spiritual master is not simply sentiment. The real substance of the spiritual master's association is his vani, his teachings. We should know what it is, feel attached to it, and serve it with our life's energy.

Satisfaction of the self-realized spiritual master is the secret of advancement in spiritual life. Inquiries and submission constitute the proper combination for spiritual understanding. Unless there is submission and service, inquires from the learned spiritual master will not be effective. Not only should one hear submissively from the spiritual master, but one must also get a clear understanding from him, in submission and service and inquiries.—Bg. 4.34, purport

Following Srila Prabhupada's Order is the Only Way to Be Guru

Srila Prabhupada said that it was not difficult to be a guru. Guru means following one's own spiritual master in parampara and repeating what Krishna has said. We have already discussed that following the spiritual master means following both his orders and his emphasis. Specifically in ISKCON this means chanting sixteen rounds of the Hare Krishna mantra every day, following the four regulative principles, and rendering service in ISKCON in the mood in which Srila Prabhupada requested. A spiritual master is not measured by the size of his aura or his capacity to generate electric shocks while he's teaching, and neither is he measured by whether or not he reveals to the disciples their individual svarupa-siddhi. The qualification is that he is always serving his spiritual master purely in thoughts, words, and deeds.

Generally, as in school, the critical student becomes the next professor. Through relevant inquiry and service (the test of his understanding) to the teacher, the student is trained to teach. Lord Caitanya Himself preaches this simple principle to Kurma Brahmana: "Instruct everyone to follow the orders of Lord Sri Krishna as they are given in Bhagavad-gita and Srimad-Bhagavatam. In this way become a spiritual master and try to liberate everyone in this land." (Cc. Madhya 7.128) Lord Caitanya goes on to say, "If you follow these regulative principles, we will again meet here, or, rather, you will never lose My company."

Srila Bhaktisiddhanta Sarasvati Thakura quoted this verse on the occasion of his Vyasa-puja in February of 1936. Srila Bhaktisiddhanta claimed that to set oneself up as a representative of God can be seen as arrogant. He said that by listening to the words of praise directed at him by his disciples, however, he was actually discharging a duty on behalf of his spiritual master:

I have therefore to practice to sit at these assemblies in the garb of a wise person and to listen to the words of praise relying on the dictum that the command of the master is above questioning. If, however, I am thereby led to suppose that it is a good thing to listen to one's own praises, my worthlessness is published to all the world in a glaring manner by such silly thinking.

I am obliged to accept this honor in order that the current of the word of God may not be obstructed and its perennial flow may not cease. Our judgment in this matter is different from that of persons who listen to their praises for pampering their arrogance by such audiencing.

In other words, accepting the role of guru in ISKCON is one of the duties Srila Prabhupada has designated for his disciples. His disciples should therefore perform this service as duty, with the aim to spread Prabhupada's fame and mission, and not to "pamper their arrogance." It was not Srila Prabhupada's mood to emphasize our own genius or spiritual status as something separate from our identity as his disciples. Therefore, our teachings should be in line from him, and we should not feel inclined to discuss topics which Srila Prabhupada himself did not discuss. Being guru in ISKCON means strictly following Srila Prabhupada's examples and remaining always his servant. Srila Prabhupada said about himself, "My credit is not that I am a great scholar or a great devotee. Neither can I perform any magic. Rather, the one qualification I have is that I have cent percent faith in my spiritual master." Srila Prabhupada did not change his own spiritual master's teachings nor emphasize those things that Bhaktisiddhanta Sarasvati Thakura chose not to emphasize. Srila Prabhupada claimed that this loyalty was the source of his power to spread the Krishna consciousness movement all over the world.

The Qualifications of Srila Prabhupada's Followers

That's the process for us to follow, but in ISKCON there have been many failures in following Prabhupada to this degree that have led to disappointment. Because Srila Prabhupada's books are nondifferent from himself, people still come to Krishna consciousness through Srila Prabhupada's preaching. People still make the commitment to chant the holy name because they have been convinced by Srila Prabhupada's encouragement. People have still decided to pursue a guru-disciple relationship based on the power that Srila Prabhupada himself displayed as a spiritual master. Even though they are joining after Srila Prabhupada's disappearance, their attraction to Srila Prabhupada and their desire to follow him are what give them solidity in their attempts to practice spiritual life.

Often devotees wonder whether because of the disappointments, it means that none of Srila Prabhupada's disciples are qualified to be gurus, or whether we should not think of another, seemingly more practical system to avoid the chance of disappointment. There is no blanket statement we can throw over this issue to say that none of Prabhupada's disciples are capable to accept disciples just because some of his disciples have failed in this regard. The point that makes them qualified is their own strict following of Srila Prabhupada. It is to Prabhupada's glory that he was able to take such raw recruits, people who had previously been eating meat and living for sense gratification and turn them into Vaishnavas. Any disciple who is strictly following Srila Prabhupada's orders has had to renounce more than just their breaking of the regulative principles. They have had to step into a whole mode of life to which they were not conditioned. They had to become childlike with Srila Prabhupada and do things they could never have imagined doing, such as going off to foreign countries to establish Krishna consciousness there. The power of their austerities and the strength of Prabhupada's blessings for their surrender have given them potency. I don't say this only looking to Srila Prabhupada's initiated disciples; that same potency is being evinced and will continue to be evinced in the present generation of his granddisciples and in generations to come. This offering of a life to Srila Prabhupada's mission is a more important qualification than any mystical qualification.

Srila Prabhupada is the Center

Since the personal identification with Srila Prabhupada is the source of every follower's potency, no one in ISKCON should dampen another devotee's attraction to Srila Prabhupada or divert it to others. Srila Prabhupada is just as accessible now as he was before his disappearance. Part of ISKCON's mood in following Prabhupada is that even though such persons must take diksha from one of Prabhupada's disciples and cannot receive diksha from Srila Prabhupada himself, Srila Prabhupada is ever the founder-acarya and thus the central focus of our branch of the sampradaya.

Our worship of Srila Prabhupada is not exaggerated. All founder-acaryas in the various sampradayas are accorded similar worship. In ISKCON's case, although it is true that we are a branch of the Gaudiya Math through Prabhupada's connection with his spiritual master, and as such, we are also part of one of the four basic lines descending from Krishna, Srila Prabhupada began something that was distinguished enough from the main branch that it became a sub-branch in itself. ISKCON is not the same as the Gaudiya Math and neither did Srila Prabhupada try to make it the same. His purpose was to apply the traditions of Gaudiya Vaishnavism to Westerners in a worldwide movement, and that included making adjustments for cultural disparities between traditional Indian Vaishnava cultural expressions and the lack of them in the West—and so many other adjustments that only a worldwide preacher such as Srila Prabhupada could understand. Those adaptations and adjustments form a part of Srila Prabhupada's emphasis, and make those who accept and identify wholeheartedly with that emphasis his followers.

To be effective, therefore, his followers have to teach and bolster faith in Srila Prabhupada and represent him effectively. Then people approaching ISKCON after Srila Prabhupada's disappearance will be grateful to have received Srila Prabhupada's association through such persons who have already been trained as Prabhupada's followers. The whole basis of their relationships in ISKCON will be that everyone is following Srila Prabhupada and helping to connect one another to the founder-acarya.

No One is Denied Srila Prabhupada's Shelter

In Vaishnava history, and particularly in the history of the Gaudiya sampradaya, there is an unbroken chain of spiritual masters. The guru's disciples become the next gurus. When people come to ISKCON post-1977, they must take diksha from one of Srila Prabhupada's followers. That is the ISKCON system, and it is based on the sampradaya tradition. We have already discussed how the initiating spiritual masters in ISKCON have the duty to humbly present Srila Prabhupada's teachings, to facilitate every ISKCON devotee's following of and association with the founder-acarya, Srila Prabhupada, and to present only what he taught strictly in parampara. Then no one will be denied a connection with the pure devotee, Srila Prabhupada, not now and not generations in the future. Srila Prabhupada will remain the diksha-guru of those he personally initiated before his disappearance and the shiksha-guru of all those who came after.

Bhakti is a science, and following the guru-parampara system is a part of that science. There is no need to invent a new system for the most basic tradition. No follower of Srila Prabhupada is being denied his shelter. Srila Prabhupada can appear in their hearts, in their dreams, in their minds, and he can imbue their following of him with his own special quality of mercy. Whatever relationship we can imagine with Srila Prabhupada as a beloved spiritual master can be experienced by all devotees regardless of what year they joined because the relationship with Srila Prabhupada is eternal.

ISKCON's Right To Its Own Integrity

One point to note is that as Srila Prabhupada expresses a certain integrity and fixedness in his following of his Guru Maharaja, and as Srila Prabhupada's followers take up that example and maintain a similar integrity and fixedness in their following of Srila Prabhupada, so ISKCON has a right to represent that integrity and fixedness without outside influence. Although ISKCON's detractors have argued that ISKCON's closed doors are a sign of weakness and politicking, ISKCON has a right to conduct its affairs according to its understanding of Srila Prabhupada's mission. It is not required to accept influence from other Vaishnavas that it feels will stress something other than what Srila Prabhupada emphasized.

Rtvik—A Pragmatic Approach?

The concept that Srila Prabhupada directly initiates followers after his disappearance is not something that he himself taught. Neither is it found in the teachings of the Gaudiya sampradaya. Neither did it appear in ISKCON in the years immediately following Srila Prabhupada's disappearance. Rather, it is a concept that made its way into ISKCON around 1985 as result of the frustration resulting from gurus falling down and abandoning their positions. The first essay to appear on this topic was by Karnamrita dasa, printed in The Vedic Village Review. His subtitle was telling and true to the experience of the times: "A Pragmatic Approach." Pragmatism means that truth is determined by whatever works best. In that essay he admitted that Srila Prabhupada had established a system, but because we were unqualified to follow that system, it would be more practical to follow something we could do.

The question is sometimes asked, "Are we limiting Srila Prabhupada in saying that he cannot initiate followers after his disappearance?" But that's not the real discussion. The question more is, "Did Srila Prabhupada teach in his books, lectures, or letters, that the ritvik system was what he wanted to establish after his disappearance?" I will not discuss the intricacies of this question here, but I will say here that Srila Prabhupada's main teaching was that the disciple becomes the next spiritual master. Our becoming guru does not put us, in our minds or anyone else's, on the level of Srila Prabhupada, but that does not mean we can avoid our responsibility to preach and to give people who come as a result of that preaching Srila Prabhupada's full shelter. The ISKCON guru's qualification is that he very carefully represents Srila Prabhupada and links his own disciples to Srila Prabhupada's teachings. Srila Prabhupada said that our love for him would be proven in our willingness to cooperate with one another to maintain his institution. Therefore, Srila Prabhupada must be the central focus.

The ISKCON Experience

That said, I have to acknowledge that ISKCON devotees have all experienced a lot of disillusionment and disappointment in regard to spiritual masters falling down. ISKCON has made mistakes. We began the worship of gurus after Prabhupada in a high-spirited way, with the mistaken idea that there were only eleven gurus selected by Srila Prabhupada and that their authority was greater than the authority of the GBC body. These gurus also accepted worship even greater than what Srila Prabhupada was offered. Those Godbrothers who were not gurus were often treated almost like disciples. In some cases, this led to a corruption that blighted ISKCON's spirit and caused confusion, and ultimately, attempts at reform.

It also gave rise to disappointed devotees searching for alternatives. Some devotees became proponents of the ritvik theory and others left ISKCON to join various branches of the Gaudiya Math.

ISKCON is still in process. We can sympathize with people looking for a radical change in the system because of our recent history, and we all want to avoid falling into the traps that caused those problems. Reform is an ongoing process. The movement needs to be brought to a greater level of purity. Leaders, and especially those taking the responsibility of accepting disciples, should be careful not to commit the same mistakes that were committed in the past. They should not claim ownership over devotees and money, and they should concentrate on making their sadhana strong and focused. They should also work to maintain the devotees' faith in their strict following of Srila Prabhupada and ultimately in Srila Prabhupada himself. Larry Shinn summarized this point nicely in his essay, "Reflections on Spiritual Leadership: The Legacy of Srila Prabhupada":

I was reminded of images of a special, holy man who, by his erudition and personal piety as well as by his traditional role, touched the lives of thousands of devotees in India, America, and around the world. I was also struck by the realization that for all of his extraordinary attributes, Prabhupada could not pass on the mantle of leadership (i.e., traditional roles) for ISKCON. As I reminisced about my interactions with Krishna gurus and devotees, which began in 1974 and intensified through the 1980s, I was struck by this realization that the traditional roles and scriptural erudition could be transmitted by teaching, but that the personal piety and deep faith that attracted devotees to Prabhupada could not.

As I reviewed my interviews with devotees from the years just following the death of Prabhupada, I came to realize that many devotees, and certainly all of the newly appointed initiating gurus, spoke with a confidence and enthusiasm about their maturing Krishna faith that was almost always grounded in scriptural authority (i.e., in reciting a Krishna text), or in Prabhupada's interpretations of those texts. It is true that some of the new gurus were noted for their ecstatic chanting or personal piety, but their claim to authority was grounded primarily in scriptural passages like those cited above. Most "new gurus" exhibited a confidence, even a cockiness, that if the scriptures said a guru was "as good as God", then it was so—forgetting that such claims must be grounded in the kind of personal humility that Prabhupada exhibited. In the early and mid–1980s, I talked with some new gurus who were exceptionally bright and erudite in scriptural argumentation but who had stopped doing sankirtana themselves even as they taught the importance of such "preaching" to new devotees. I met other new gurus who were talented organizational managers but who had stopped chanting their morning rounds of japa, and ultimately fell from their lofty positions because of immoral behavior. I met only a few new gurus who were impressive because of their humbleness and piety, and they have continued to provide leadership for ISKCON—even in the dark days of the early and mid-1980s.

What is the legacy that Prabhupada has left for ISKCON? It is the legacy of traditional authority (parampara), scriptural erudition and personal piety as necessary corollaries to a healthy and vibrant Krishna faith. Even as the reformers in ISKCON attempted in the mid-1980s to reduce ISKCON's reliance on relatively few gurus (by appointing many new ones) and to separate some managerial and organizational functions from the spiritual role of the guru, Prabhupada's legacy of personal piety and moral purity seldom was offered as the key to a new guru's success. Prabhupada's legacy is a faith marked by a blend of head and heart—both focused upon God's divine mercy and compassion—that separates the true spiritual master from the impostor.

The good news is that there are many signs in America, Europe and elsewhere in the world that gurus and other leaders in ISKCON recognize that they must live and act in ways that are more consistent with their teachings. Conferences held in Europe during the past half dozen years reveal a more contrite and apologetic tone in public self-presentations by devotees. However, Prabhupada's legacy is richer still in the lesson it would teach to contemporary devotees: that the quality of one's spiritual practice and growth must undergird one's theological and scriptural erudition and public and private actions. His lesson is for the developing spiritual seeker—not for one seeking a religious role in ISKCON as an institution.

In the final analysis, Prabhupada's life suggests that only the guru who truly is linked to Krishna by his or her own private and public devotion can serve as a conduit for disciples who rely upon the Vaishnava's disciplic succession. Over the years, many Krishna devotees have quoted to me numerous scriptural passages that confirm this view of their disciplic authority—but seldom have they cited the faith-development of Prabhupada as a model for their own development. With Prabhupada, the recitation of scriptural authorities was not really necessary to confirm his role as acarya. Images of the love-filled and ecstatic Prabhupada softly singing praises to Krishna is his legacy of God-centered love—images which can serve ISKCON and its leaders well in his absence. It is this legacy of a guru's devotion and humility before God—his piety—that Prabhupada asks his successors to emulate. What better legacy could a spiritual teacher leave to those who would follow him?

Ultimately, what ISKCON's devotees want to do is not to leave ISKCON or take up the banner of things not taught by Prabhupada in their disappointment. Rather, they want to get back to Prabhupada. This requires working from within the movement to effect reform. The GBC should also be open to discussing reform. But the process will not be effective in an environment of rebellion or anarchy. ISKCON needs leadership because it is a large organization. Srila Prabhupada's ambitious plan to influence the world toward the bhakti path seems almost impossible to realize, but this was the desire of the compassionate Vaishnava. His methods of realizing that goal included book distribution, temple maintenance, educational programs, prasadam distribution, and the elevation of those followers who had already joined. All of these projects require organization. To contend with opposition, both internal and external, also requires organization and singlemindedness. We have to protect ourselves, through laws and regulation, from undue internal competition or misunderstanding. The society's individual branches must be able to maintain their integrity and yet share the same vision as all other centers. Only by such organization can we assure that no individual member becomes corrupt and tries to mislead the whole mission. The GBC is an important feature of this organization.

Therefore, it is vital that the GBC become responsive to the body of devotees and that the body of devotees cooperate within the system. Together, we can go forward both in developing our internal Krishna consciousness and in carrying out Srila Prabhupada's mission. Allegiance to ISKCON is a way of expressing allegiance to Srila Prabhupada. We should not think of ourselves as lone aspiring Vaishnavas in the world but as Prabhupada's followers, interested in maintaining, improving, and expanding his mission. Doing so from whatever position we find ourselves in life, whether living inside the temple or outside, single or married, is our testimony of our love and faith in Srila Prabhupada. We all recognize that our movement is imperfect. As Srila Bhaktivinoda Thakura states, "Nothing is pure in the beginning. From impurity, purity will come about." Our movement will be rescued not by abandoning it or by changing Srila Prabhupada's teachings but by becoming the devotees Prabhupada wanted us to be and by sharing that example and that happiness with the world. © Satsvarupa dasa Goswami

TAKING SRILA PRABHUPADA STRAIGHT

(Excerpts)

by His Grace Ravindra Svarupa Prabhu

A mature Prabhupada disciple who had spent several years with Narayana Maharaja and his followers but has now become disillusioned, reports having directly heard Narayana Maharaja vow to reinitiate the disciples of ISKCON gurus, "I'll reinitiate their disciples!"

In 1990 I was persuaded by some who were then taking siksa from Narayana Maharaja to visit him. In the course of our discussion, the invocation of Sri Isopanisad somehow came up, and I rendered the meaning and purport the way it was presented by Srila Prabhupada, mentioning that this world ('idam'), as an emanation from the 'purnam', is also 'purnam'.

Narayana Maharaja immediately cut me off, and pronounced (in quite an ex cathedra manner) that I understood the text incorrectly. "No!" he said. "The material world is not purnam." 'Idam' did not refer to this material world, which cannot be purnam. Rather, he said, 'idam' refers to Visnu-tattva expansions like Balarama. They are purnam.

I was a bit shocked. Here I was Prabhupada's disciple, yet he was telling me Prabhupada was in error in his books. Of course, I understood at once that Narayana Maharaja had to be ignorant of Prabhupada's books. He had not been enlightened by Prabhupada's brilliant account of just what it meant for this material world to be realized as a complete whole. (It seemed weird to give an interpretation that ignored the context of the invocation, and to ignore the fact that everywhere in the Upanisads and the Bhagavatam 'idam' is conventionally used to stand for 'this world'; and how strange it is to use a neuter singular pronoun to refer to Balarama and other expansions. To give him the benefit of the doubt, I assume he had some authority for his gloss of the sruti mantra. At any rate, Prabhupada's understanding is clearly far more profound. I actually felt sorry for Narayana Maharaja that he had not received the benefit of Prabhupada's teaching.)

Didn't Prabhupada emphasize the importance of his books for us? Didn't he tell us that association with him via his books was better than his personal association? Now, how is a person who has never even bothered to read Prabhupada's books to be considered his siksa disciple? How is he to represent Prabhupada to us? Narayana Maharaja announced himself as the successor-acarya to Prabhupada, the authorized acarya of ISKCON.

Two years ago, Lokanatha Swami brought ISKCON's parikrama party to Kesavji Gaudiya Math in Mathura, where Narayana Maharaja addressed them. It became quite emotional. He said that he used to "lie under the Tamal tree" and to "rest his head in the lap of Giriraja." He said that even Lokanatha Swami used to be his friend. But all of them left him. They deserted him.

And then, when the parikrama party had left, Narayana Maharaja turned to his disciples and said, "Not one of these is a true follower of Srila Prabhupada! I am the only true follower of Srila Prabhupada!" Other witnesses have heard him voice the same idea still more recently: "I am the successor to Srila Prabhupada," he says. Even: "I am ISKCON."

There was a time when Narayana Maharaja criticized Prabhupada in public. He pointed out "mistakes" in his books and "mistakes" in naming of certain Deities. Now, however, he claims that he never said these were Prabhupada's mistakes but those of his followers, and he never criticized Prabhupada. This is not true. The truth is that in private Narayana Maharaja still belittles or criticizes Prabhupada, while praising him in public. And if the private is made public he simply denies it happened.

If we were to accept Narayana Maharaja's claims, we would be disregarding Prabhupada's explicit directions to us, and, in so doing, reenacting the error of the Gaudiya Matha in disobeying the orders of its founder-acarya. Prabhupada's instructions to us are clear and open and direct, and he has warned us of the folly of deviating from them:

> *Why this Gaudiya Matha failed? Because they tried to become more than guru. He, before passing away, he gave all direction and never said that 'This man should be the next acarya.' But these people, just after his passing away they began to fight, who shall be acarya. That is the failure. They never thought, 'Why Guru Maharaja gave us instruction so many things, why he did not say that this man should be acarya?' They wanted to create artificially somebody acarya and everything failed. They did not consider even with common sense that if Guru Maharaja wanted to appoint somebody as acarya, why did he not say? He said so many things, and this point he missed? The real point? And they insist upon it. They declared some unfit person to become acarya. Then another man came, then another, acarya, another acarya. So better remain a foolish person perpetually to be directed by Guru Maharaja. That is perfection.* (Srila Prabhupada Speaking in a Room conversation, Bombay: August 16, 1976)

What would it be like to stand before Srila Prabhupada and explain on what authority Narayana Maharaja is to be promoted as our next acarya?

DEVIATIONS

Srila Bhaktisiddhanta Sarasvati Thakura Prabhupada radically reformed the Gaudiya Tradition, transforming it into a global preaching mission for the modern world. His work was not much appreciated by many, prominent among them the babajis of Vraja, who felt that he was deviating by his emphasis on vigorous preaching rather than the esoteric cultivation of raga-marga. His disciples were constantly assailed by the charge that their Guru Maharaja was a deviant who could not offer them the "real thing." As you know, a number of them succumbed, most prominently the unauthorized "successor-acarya" Ananta Vasudeva dasa (later reinitiated in the babaji community as Puri Goswami).

A number of our own God-brothers also fell prey to the same attack, even while Prabhupada was present. What Narayana Maharaja is now preaching and delivering clearly comes from outside the line of Bhaktisiddhanta Sarasvati Thakura. He did not get this from Bhakti Prajnan Kesava Maharaja, his diksa guru. Narayana Maharaja has acknowledged that there was no practice of raga marga in that matha, no "rasa-katha" but rather discourse about Prahlada Maharaja, Dhruva Maharaja, and so on.

Narayana Maharaja was apparently not satisfied with this, for, as he once confessed, he left his spiritual master's temple without permission, and he went to Govardhana. In great distress, crying, Bhakti Prajnan Kesava Maharaja came and brought him back.

But later, after the departure of his Guru Maharaja, Narayana Maharaja returned to the babajis of Govardhana, and from among them he accepted a rasika guru, supposedly the one who "pushed the switch" which made the "current of bhava flow." After his guru's departure Narayana Maharaja did something his guru had forcibly prohibited in his presence. Whatever it is that Narayana Maharaja is giving comes from this babaji. This is his lineage. It is clearly not the lineage from Bhaktisiddhanta Sarasvati Thakura.

In Vrndavana there are prakrta-sahajiyas who say that writing books or even touching books is taboo. For them, devotional service means being relieved from these activities. Whenever they are asked to hear a recitation of Vedic literature, they refuse, saying, "What business do we have reading or hearing transcendental literatures? They are meant for neophytes." However, pure devotees under the guidance of Srila Rupa Gosvami reject this sahajiya philosophy. It is certainly not good to write literature for money or reputation, but to write books and publish them for the enlightenment of the general populace is real service to the Lord. That was Srila Bhaktisiddhanta Sarasvati's opinion, and he specifically told his disciples to write books. He actually preferred to publish books rather than establish temples. According to Bhaktisiddhanta Sarasvati Thakura, distributing literature is like playing on a great mrdanga. Consequently we always request members of the International Society for Krishna Consciousness to publish as many books as possible and distribute them widely throughout the world. By thus following in the footsteps of Srila Rupa Gosvami, one can become a rupanuga devotee.

Narayana Maharaja once said that the result of book distribution by a member of ISKCON would be that in his next life the book distributor might qualify for advanced association (of a rasika bhakta), but that was all. Yet Srila Prabhupada did not recognize such a dichotomy between Gauranga's seva and Gopijanavallabha's seva, for, as he famously commented: "Book distribution is in the mood of the gopis." Srila Prabhupada tells us that he attained this realization from his Guru Maharaja, Srila Bhaktisiddhanta Sarasvati Thakura (Madhya 19.133, Purport)

In this connection, I am enclosing an exact (unedited) typescript of Prabhupada's preface to the original edition of the second volume of Srimad Bhagavatam (1964). Here, Prabhupada replies to criticisms of his activity. These very same criticisms of "brhat-mrdanga preaching," voiced by the sahajiya babajis of Vraja, are unfortunately being recycled by Narayana Maharaja.

Prabhupada begins by saying:

> The path of fruitive activities i.e. to say the path of earn money and enjoy life as it is going on generally, — appears to have become also our

> profession although we have renounced the order of worldly life! They see that we are moving in the cities, in the Government offices, banks and other business places for promoting the publication of Srimad Bhagwatam. They also see that we are moving in the press, paper market and amongst the book binders also away from our residence at Vrindaban and thus they conclude sometimes mistakenly that we are also doing the same business in the dress of a mendicant!

And Srila Prabhupada winds up by voicing his heart-felt conviction:

> So even though we are not in the Himalayas, even though we talk of business, even though we deal in rupees and n.P. still, simply because we are 100 per cent servants of the Lord and are engaged in the service of broadcasting the message of His glories, — certainly we shall transcend and get through the invincible impasse of Maya and reach the effulgent kingdom of God to render Him face to face eternal service, in full bliss and knowledge. We are confident of this factual position and we may also assure to our numerous readers that they will also achieve the same result simply by hearing the glories of the Lord. (Jannama sruti matrena puman bhavati nirmala.)

Narayana Maharaja explains Prabhupada's high praise for book distribution and book distributors as a mere tactic to encourage those of us without the samskara for raga-marga. Therefore it is worth noting that this preface was written about his own activities and some years before he had any neophytes to encourage.

During Kartika last year, Narayana Maharaja was holding a darsana in which a number of disciples of Gaura Govinda Maharaja were present. He announced that last night Gaura Govinda Maharaja had appeared to him in a dream, and after speaking some words, Gaura Govinda Maharaja merged into Narayana Maharaja's body.

Srila Prabhupada said:

> *Therefore those who are sahajiyas, they simply go to the pastimes of Lord Krsna with the gopis. Other things: "Oh, no, no. That is not Krsna's pastimes. That is not Krsna's pastimes." That is, they differentiate the absolute activities of the Absolute. That is called sahajiya. The sahajiyas will never read Bhagavad-gita, will never read. [Sarcastically:] Because they have been elevated to the mellows of conjugal love. Therefore they have no interest in Bhagavad-gita.* (Lecture on Srimad-Bhagavatam 6.3.20-23; Gorakhpur, February 14, 1971)

Narayana Maharaja says within smaller circles that he has no taste for Bhagavad-gita, no attraction for Puri or Dvaraka, no interest in Rama or Narasingha.

SUMMARY

We can begin to understand what influence Narayana Maharaja exercise to make devotees disobey Srila Prabhupada? Let us look at the reason Satsvarupa Maharaja stopped hearing from Narayana Maharaja. He was the first of ISKCON leaders to reject Narayana Maharaja as a teacher. When a crisis arose concerning the others who continued under his tutelage, I asked Satsvarupa Maharaja what made him decide to quit.

He told me, "I discovered that I was reading Srila Prabhupada through the eyes of Narayana Maharaja. And I decided I had better take my Srila Prabhupada straight."

Now, I accept Satsvarupa Maharaja's account. He is by nature transparently honest—even, some say, to a fault. His own account is characteristically direct, simple and guileless. Satsvarupa Maharaja noticed how some subtle and powerful change was happening in his hearing of Prabhupada, and Prabhupada was now coming to him in a distorted or crooked manner. He was hearing Prabhupada differently, and this gave him such qualms that he took remedial measures.

According to Narayana Maharaja, Prabhupada was, in effect, a lower-level guru (a teacher of vaidhi-bhakti only) while Narayana Maharaja is a higher-level guru (a giver of raga-marga). In essence, then, those who follow him may set aside significant parts of Srila Prabhupada's teachings and directions as a kind of outgrown elementary instruction. In effect, Narayana Maharaja gives them the way to "respectfully" disregard Srila Prabhupada's teachings without suffering the pang of conscience.

I doubt Narayana Maharaja's claims to be Prabhupada's follower or designated successor because A) he acts in an envious manner toward Vaisnavas and ISKCON in particular and seems to be driven by a competitive spirit of domination, B) he is unacquainted with Prabhupada's teachings and he differs from them in many ways, C) he has gone outside the line of Bhaktisiddhanta Sarasvati Thakura for instruction and does not follow the directions given by Bhaktisiddhanta Sarasvati Thakura and D) he receives teachings on "raga-marga" from babajis unauthorizedly.

GBC ON "PROMINENT LINK"

A Preliminary Statement from ISKCON's Governing Body Commission

"Srila Prabhupada: The Prominent Link" written by Dhira Govinda Prabhu has fundamental inconsistencies with Srila Prabhupada's teachings. Although the work encourages Srila Prabhupada's pre-eminence in ISKCON, it does so in a concocted way. As disciples of Srila Prabhupada, we cannot endorse anything different from what he taught, no matter how it may appeal to sentiment.

Out of respect for the author, the GBC Body requests its Sastric Advisory Council to review the paper and comment on it more deeply. For now, to protect devotees from being misled, the GBC Body offers these specific examples of how "The Prominent Link" deviates from Srila Prabhupada's teachings and instructions.

- The paper begins by improperly dismissing the standard terminology of *siksa* and *diksa guru* – terminology established by Lord Caitanya Himself and followed by all prominent *acharyas*. Srila Prabhupada uses *siksa* and *diksa* as essential words to define functions of specific gurus. The author, by contrast, calls them "appellations" and "labels" and discards them.

- Having discarded the terms, the author attempts to merge the functions of *siksa* and *diksa* gurus. Noting that Srila Prabhupada is ISKCON's pre-eminent instructing guru, he writes, "it is questionable whether the devotee performing the initiation ceremony can unambiguously be termed '<u>the</u> *diksa* guru.'" Srila Prabhupada, by contrast, states unambiguously in the *Krishna* book, Chapter 80, (and elsewhere): "*Siksa* gurus may be many, but *diksa* guru is always one."

- Srila Prabhupada exhorted his disciples hundreds of times to be the next gurus in disciplic succession by simply repeating what they heard and avoiding concoctions. Why would he do so if he intended to be directly responsible for initiating future generations? Srila Prabhupada explains, "One's guide must be a spiritual master who is . . . strictly following the instructions of the previous acarya . . . ." *(CC Madhya 10.17*, purport*)*.

- "The Prominent Link" specifically contradicts Srila Prabhupada's own description of his relationship with initiates of those he initiated. On May 28, 1977, in a conversation with the GBC in Vrndavana, he said those devotees would be his "grand disciples" and "the disciples of my disciples." Disciples of Srila Prabhupada's disciples are in fact directly connected to him through initiation as his grand-disciples. Srila Prabhupada commented that the grandfather is more kind to his grandchildren than is their father. There is nothing lacking in the connection between Srila Prabhupada and his grand disciples. Some may choose to emphasize their *diksa* guru and others their *siksa* guru. Such affairs of the heart cannot be legislated by anyone.

- In the same conversation Srila Prabhupada described those who would be taking on the service of initiating disciples as "regular gurus." The "Prominent Link" terms them "Vaishnavas who perform the initiation ceremony." Further, the work fails to offer a single statement by Srila Prabhupada in support of the implication that His Divine Grace would serve – in any respect – as a *diksa* guru in posthumous initiations.

- "The Prominent Link" suggests that if every member of ISKCON makes Srila Prabhupada the "sole object of unconditional surrender," ISKCON will be more united. Srila Prabhupada's teachings suggest that ISKCON will be more united – and Srila Prabhupada more pleased – if every member of ISKCON serves the servants of the servants of Srila Prabhupada: "This is called parampara system. You have to learn how to become servant of the servant of Krsna. The more you become in the lower position — servant, servant, servant, servant, servant, hundreds times servant, servant — the more you are advanced. Here in this material world everyone is trying to be master of the master. Just opposite. And the spiritual world, the endeavor is to become servant's servant. This is the secret. *yasya deve para bhaktir yatha deve tatha gurau/ tasyaite kathita hy arthah prakasante mahatmanah*. This is Vedic instruction" (London, 8/3/73).

ISKCON Law establishes Srila Prabhupada as the "pre-eminent and compulsory *siksa* guru for all members of ISKCON." Further, it says that any grand disciple may find more inspiration from Srila Prabhupada than from their *diksa* guru. "The Prominent Link" asserts that such understandings of Srila Prabhupada are offensive to His Divine Grace (p. 26). The GBC Body finds such remarks and their public circulation wanting in scholarship, philosophy, and Vaishnava etiquette.

Since Srila Prabhupada entered samadhi, his disciples have struggled to properly establish *guru-tattva* in ISKCON, and there is more to be done. In that respect the GBC Body acknowledges the overt intent of "The Prominent Link." Unfortunately, the paper fails in its attempt to glorify Srila Prabhupada owing to an incomplete consideration of his teachings or, worse, a willingness to take a little from here, and little from there, and create something new. The result is *aviddhi purvakam* an improper method of worshipping Srila Prabhupada.

The GBC Body acknowledges with appreciation the clarification offered by Dhira Govinda Prabhu in a letter (March 2002) in which he states that he did not intend to teach ritvikism nor support the ritvik agenda through "The Prominent Link." He also expressed his eagerness to enter into further discussion with the GBC and its Sastric Advisory Council.

Thus the GBC Body encourages Dhira Govinda Prabhu to give serious consideration to the discrepancies mentioned here – and others that can be raised – and discuss them with its Sastric Advisory Council.
March 12, 2002

Contributing to this paper: Drutakarma dasa, Hridayananda dasa Goswami, Kalakantha dasa, and Ravindra Svarupa dasa.

FROM UPAPATI SWAMI TO PROMINENT LINK AUTHOR

I am disturbed by your presentation of the initiating spiritual master as more of a big brother than a spiritual master. You are, in effect, inventing a new kind of spiritual master, different from what is presented in shastra and in Srila Prabhupada's books.

It is true that the spiritual master must represent the disciplic succession, and I present myself to my disciples as the representative of Srila Prabhupada. Still, I am more than a big brother. It has to be that way or they will simply try to understand by their speculation and arrive at impersonalist conclusions.

There have been times when I screamed at the top of my lungs and brought grown men to tears to impress upon them that they had committed an offense by presenting Srila Prabhupada's teachings as impersonalism. It is not my usual method of teaching, but the disciples in question later expressed their gratitude to me for doing it.

I could not have done this, however, if I were simply the kind of big-brother spiritual master that you propose. They would have simply continued in their speculation in spite of my pleading. In fact, I have seen that people who do not wholeheartedly accept the authority of the spiritual master end up mired in endless speculation.

You do not have disciples, so you cannot understand the situation from the point of view of one who has accepted this responsibility. And it is a grave responsibility. The fact that some have been remiss in the pursuance of this responsibility, however, does not justify changing the essential nature of the guru-disciple relationship as given to us by Lord Krsna and Srila Prabhupada.

CHAPTER 4: POETRY

SRILA PRABHUPADA'S REMNANTS

(A vyasa-puja offering from Adi Purusa dasa)

nama om visnu padaya krishna presthaya bhu tale
srimate bhaktivedanta swamin iti namine

namas te sarasvati deve gaura vani pracarine
nirvisesa sunyavaadi pascatya desa tarine

Dear Srila Prabhupada,

I have never written to you before. Your good disciple, Sri Padmalocana prabhu, is inspiring us to rise above our lethargy and try to offer some expression of gratitude to you, especially on this most auspicious occasion of the 106th anniversary of your appearance in this world.

You have shown the highest compassion by coming to save us from hell, and your disciples, sharing in that compassion, are passing it down to the next generation, eager that we not miss out on the gift that you are giving.

I offer myself at the lotus feet of your servant, and then with his permission I may try to offer some humble words of appreciation for the savior of the whole world.

Of course you are watching us. We are your children and grandchildren. You were watching when I first stumbled upon your Bhāgavata Gita As It Is, and when I first started thumbing through the pages with delighted curiosity, not at all aware of what was to come.

You were there in that small but perfect ISKCON center when I first tasted Krishna's prasadam and chanted His holy names in sankirtana. You saw that spark of fascination in my heart and you fanned it. You brought that irresistible sweetness. It was all new to me, but I knew that it was all coming from you, the person who wrote the book that I loved. And it was all just as sweet. How could I not come back? I would keep coming back.

You saw my suffering condition even when I did not, and you were watching my first crude attempts to live my life in a nice way, a pure way, according to what I had learned by your mercy.

You knew my heart and you were my only hope, back in those days when

I first tried to do my work for the pleasure of Krishna, even though I was still entangled in a world of sinful people... when I tried to chant the holy names of Krishna with a head full of LSD . It was a cry in the wilderness, from the depths of ignorance. But you heard, Srila Prabhupada. You were with me then.

And only by your grace did I ever get free from those unwanted things, and only by your grace will I ever get free from the faults which bind me now.

You came in my dream the first night that I slept in an ISKCON center, and I chanted Hare Krishna with you. Later in your place at 26 2nd Ave I felt your reassuring presence. I was in the right place and your movement was for everyone, even for people like me.

And your disciples have accepted me, by your grace. I try to help them because they are serving you. I follow them because they follow you.

You left some water for me. Jaya Murari Prabhu gave me some remnants from your last cup of water. 20 years later. Then I drank it and I ran to tell Visvaretah, your disciple.

"I just drank Srila Prabhupada's remnants!"

"Adi Purusa, this whole movement is Srila Prabhupada's remnants."

Your movement: your books, your temples, your devotees— your Krishna.
This is our life. You have given us life and our life is for you.
We can never repay you, but we can preach vigorously.
Please keep me.

Adi Purusa das
servant of your servant
useless though I may be

DOORS

By Yamunacarya dasa Vanacari

I withhold and send forth the rain. I am immortality and I am also death personified. Both spirit and matter are in Me."

—*Bhagavad-gita*, 9:19

Krishna lets us enter as we choose.
Thoughts of Him direct just where we go.
The droughts, storms and bruises that we know should
never be surprising news.

For as we enter, so we must depart,
and whether we trudge back to troubled flesh
or wake to spirit unimaginably fresh
reflects just how we hold Him in our heart.

Through love we can give mad mind its ease,
when we depend for everything on, Him,
or rather lean on frenzied human whim
as false shelter fails, and freeze.

Matter dies and spirit never does.
Material muck lugs its doomed desires.
Why be bound with senses' prattling liars
wailing for what never was?

Endless wonder finds the soul
that longs for God and infinite exchange
and wishes just to glorify the range
of love in He who inhabits all.

And so we circle or move on.
It's deathless either way.
We can lust and suffer here and stay,
or celebrate that craving,
grief (and all their fears) are gone.

For this we must let go our link
with every false, gross and greedy fear
that traps our burdened consciousness here
and learn to love what He Who loves us thinks.

CHAPTER 5: PHILOSOPHY

LORD CAITANYA

ONCE IN A DAY OF BRAHMA

Lord Gauranga Mahaprabhu appears to preach Krishna consciousness in that particular Kali-yuga directly following the Dvapara-yuga in which the Supreme Personality of Godhead Lord Sri Krishna appears. The two special yugas wherein Lord Krishna and Lord Caitanya appear are called svatantra. Lord Krishna and Lord Caitanya don't appear in every Dvapara and Kali-yuga...Krishna and Gauranga perform their transcendental pastimes only once in a day of Lord Brahma. During the reign of the Vaivasvata manvantara, Lord Syamasundara came as Lord Gauranga. Lord Gauranga worships Lord Krishna, the Lord of Dvapara, by doing Hari-nama sankirtana." In previous Kali yugas the Supreme Lord came in the form of Lord Narayana.

(Caitanya Mangala; Locana dasa Thakura p.87-89 Spoken by a brahmana at the time of Lord Caitanya's brahminical initiation)

SENAPATI BHAKTA

Even if the sinners reject religion or flee to foreign countries, still they will get the mercy. I will send mor senapati bhakta to go there and deliver them. *(Caitanya Mangala by Locana dasa Thakura p. 44; Lord Caitanya speaking to His associates in Goloka;) [mor means My; senapati means a military field commander, and bhakta means a devotee. So Lord Caitanya will empower His own devotee to spread Krishna consciousness aroud the world.]*

SON OF SACI

ajayadhvamaja yadhvam na sansayah
kalau sankirtana rambhe bhavisyami saci sutah

The Supreme Lord said, "In Kali-yuga, I will appear as the son of Saci, and inaugurate the sankirtana movement. There is no doubt about this.

(Caitanya Mangala, p.38; From Bhavisya Purana quoted by Lord Brahma to Narada)

NAVADVIPA AND GOLOKA

See Caitanya Mangala, p. 20 describes talk between Narada, Uddhava, Rukmini, etc. quoted by Murari Gupta to Damodara Pandita wriiten by Locana dasa Thakura; see Jaiminiya Bharata 32 chapter, Asvamedha Parva.

In the Veda it is also said, "Let me tell you the mystery. In Navadvīpa, the identical realm of Goloka, on the bank of the Ganges, Gauracandra who is Govinda, the entity of pure cognition, who has two hands, who is the soul of all souls, who has the supreme great personality as the great meditative sannyāsin and who is beyond the threefold mundane attributes, makes the process of pure unalloyed devotion manifest in this mundane world. He is sole Godhead. He is the source of all forms, the Supreme Soul and is Godhead manifesting Himself in yellow, red, blue and white colors. He is the direct entity of pure cognition full of the spiritual (cit) potency. He is the figure of the devotee. He is the bestower of devotion and cognizable by devotion alone. The selfsame Gauracandra, who is no other than Kṛṣṇa Himself, in order to taste the rasa of the pastimes of Rādhā-Kṛṣṇa in Goloka, is manifest in the eternal realm of Navadvīpa identical with Goloka." This is also clear from the Vedic declarations, viz., āsan varṇās trayaḥ, kṛṣṇa-varṇaṁ tviṣākṛṣṇam, yathā paśyaḥ paśyati rukma-varṇam, mahān prabhur vai and various other statements of the theistic scriptures. Just as Śrī Kṛṣṇa had His birth in the mundane Gokula through the agency of Yogamāyā who is the primal energy of the Supreme Lord, so with her help He manifests the līlā of His birth in the womb of Śacī-devī in Navadvīpa on this mundane plane. These are the absolute truths of spiritual science and not the outcome of imaginary speculation under the thraldom of the deluding energy of Godhead. (Brahma Samhita 5.6 Purport by Srila Bhaktisiddhanta Sarasvati Goswami)

INTERESTING ANECDOTES

KRSNA GIVES LIBERATION

When killed by Lord Visṇu, the demon Kālanemi did not attain liberation, but again appeared in the material world as King Kaṁsa. When that same demon was again killed by Lord Kṛsṇa, the same demon immediately became liberated. From this account we may understand that demons directly killed by Lord Kṛsṇa immediately attain liberation, although demons killed by Lord Visnu, or other forms of the Lord, do not necessarily attain liberation. By this we may see the singular power and greatness of Lord Kṛṣṇa. (Krsna Sandharba: Annuceda 73.4: Srila Jiva Gosvami)

BUDDHISM AND SOUL

The voidist philosophy of Buddha had already practically destroyed the teachings of the Vedas and the duties of varnasrama-dharma. Voidist Buddhism even denied the existence of the Supreme Personality of Godhead. Although it did hint at the existence of the individual soul, Buddhism denied the soul's true eternal nature.(Jaiva Dharma Ch. 2:)

BHAKTISIDDHANTA

He was never interested in such activities as bathing in the ocean at Puri or in holy rivers, which he considered to be a diversion from his life's engagement of absorption in bhajan, hearing, chanting, preaching, and writing. (From Bhaktisiddhanta: part 1, pg. 30—Bhaktivikasa Swami)

DYING IN HOLY PLACE

Hari-śauri: You saw him in Bombay last year. He had just done some drawings for the development of Bhubaneshwar, and you asked him if he would like... Oh, Haridaspur. At that time he was working on some plans for Haridaspur, and you asked him if he would like to stay there. He's... Bhāgavata put that he had died of some brain virus.

Prabhupāda: In Bhubaneshwar?

Hari-śauri: Yes. That is part of Jagannātha Purī dhāma?

Prabhupāda: Oh, yes.

Hari-śauri: Is that a guarantee for going home, if someone leaves their body in the dhāma?

Prabhupāda: At least, he gets high standard of life for many years. That is stated in the Bhagavad-gītā. Find out in Bhagavad-gītā.

Hari-śauri: (pause) Prāpya puṇya-kṛtāṁ lokān?

Prabhupāda: Hm.

Hari-śauri:

uṣitvā śāśvatīḥ samāḥ
śucīnāṁ śrīmatāṁ gehe
yoga-bhraṣṭo 'bhijāyate

Prabhupāda: Read the whole verse.

Hari-śauri: The English?

Prabhupāda: Or Sanskrit.

Hari-śauri: That was text 41. "The unsuccessful yogi, after many, many years of enjoyment on the planets of the pious living entities, is born into a family of righteous people or into a family of rich aristocracy." Then the next verse,

athavā yoginām eva
kule bhavati dhīmatām
etad dhi durlabhataraṁ
loke janma yad īdṛśam

"Or he takes his birth in a family of transcendentalists, who are surely great in wisdom. Verily, such a birth is rare in this world."

tatra taṁ buddhi-saṁyogaṁ
labhate paurva-dehikam
yatate ca tato bhūyaḥ
saṁsiddhau kuru-nandana

"On taking such a birth, he again revives the divine consciousness of his previous life, and he tries to make further progress in order to achieve complete success, O son of Kuru." [break] ...telegram came today. It didn't give the exact time, but it came from Bhubaneshwar.

Prabhupāda: He was there?

Hari-śauri: Yes. He was working with Gaura-Govinda Mahārāja.

Prabhupāda: He is... He was coming from Australia. (Room Conversation — October 25, 1977, Vṛndāvana)

BIBLE, MEAT EATING & IDOLS

Says doesn't matter what you eat, but shouldn't eat meat if it causes a brother to fall. Shouldn't eat food sacrificed to idols. (See Corinthians 8)

DHRUVALOKA

Lord Vishnu said, "You'll achieve the topmost post in the three worlds. You, the son of Uttanapada, will become the king, and all your subjects will receive My favor. Your abode will be called Dhruvaloka, which will be located above all the planets of the sages.'

After saying this, Vishnu disappeared. On the Lord's order, Visvakarma built Dhruvaloka. Upon receiving this boon, Dhruva started for home." (Caitanya Maṅgala; Madhya Khanda; Ch. 11 p.205)

DON'T DISCOURAGE FROM WORK?

TRANSLATION: The people in general are naturally inclined to enjoy, and you have encouraged them in that way in the name of religion. This is verily condemned and is quite unreasonable. Because they are guided under your instructions, they will accept such activities in the name of religion and will hardly care for prohibitions.

PURPORT: In histories like the Mahābhārata, of course, there are topics on transcendental subjects along with material topics. The Bhagavad-gītā is there in the Mahābhārata. The whole idea of the Mahābhārata culminates in the ultimate instructions of the Bhagavad-gītā, that one should relinquish all other engagements and should engage oneself solely and fully in surrendering unto the lotus feet of Lord Śrī Kṛṣṇa. But men with materialistic tendencies are more attracted to the politics, economics and philanthropic activities mentioned in the Mahābhārata than to the principal topic, namely the Bhagavad-gītā. This compromising spirit of Vyāsadeva is directly condemned by Nārada, who advises him to directly proclaim that the prime necessity of human life is to realize one's eternal relation with the Lord and thus surrender unto Him without delay.

A patient suffering from a particular type of malady is almost always inclined to accept eatables which are forbidden for him. The expert physician does not make any compromise with the patient by allowing him to take partially what he should not at all take. In the Bhagavad-gītā it is also said that a man attached to fruitive work should not be discouraged from his occupation, for gradually he may be elevated to the position of self-realization. This is sometimes applicable for those who are only dry empiric philosophers without spiritual realization. But those who are in the devotional line need not be always so advised. (SB 1.5.15)

NOT LOOSE IN OUR CAMPUS

And in our, this campus, actually those who are eager to advance in Kṛṣṇa consciousness, they should live, nobody else. We give free food, free apartment, cloth and everything. "Come here. Live. As far as possible we shall provide." But this is specially meant for bhagavad-bhajana. Attend ārati, early rise in the morning, attend the functions, take prasādam... In this way everything will be reorganized, not loose things. Then what is the use of...? We have got such a... And so far the tenants are concerned, if it is possible, give them money; let them go. One, two, some have gone, and others... This whole campus should be for devotees. We don't want tenant. And it should be developed for that purpose, for developing Kṛṣṇa consciousness. Either here or outside India or anywhere, this principle should be followed. And this hodgepodge association, society, is not the... Let it be very pure. Ekaś candras tamo hanti na ca tārā. That one moon is sufficient. There is no need of millions of stars. Hm? What do you think? One moon gives light. So, in this way, if we can make one person really Kṛṣṇa conscious, then our mission is successful.

What is the use of millions of stars twinkling? What is called? Twinkling? You should discuss all these things, (Room Conversation — January 7, 1977, Bombay)

MAYAVADI'S INCREASE POPULATION

At one time the demons had taken to following the path of devotion in order to fulfill their own sinful lusty desires. Seeing this the merciful Supreme Personality of Godhead, concerned for the benefit of the true, sincere devotees decided to deter the demons from following the path of devotion. With this in mind, He called for Lord Siva and told him, O Siva, that the demons in the mode of ignorance are now preaching the path of pure devotional service is not good for the world. Please write a book to bewilder the demons. Conceal the truth about Me and preach the Māyāvāda, impersonal philosophy. The demons will then leave the path of pure devotional service and take shelter of impersonalism. That will be very pleasing to My genuine pure devotees. Of this there is no doubt. The great Vaisnava Siva unhappily accepted this order of the Supreme Lord. However, he placed the Lord's order on his head and obediently preached the Māyāvāda philosophy. How can there be any fault, then, for Lord Siva, the spiritual master of the entire world? (Jaiva Dharma, ch. 18)

In the Padma Purāṇa it is stated that the Personality of Godhead ordered His Lordship Śiva to deviate the human race from Him (the Personality of Godhead). The Personality of Godhead was to be so covered so that people would be encouraged to generate more and more population. (SB Introduction)

Consequently, the impersonalist philosophers have given indirect impetus to the abominable mundane sex life because they have overstressed the impersonality of the ultimate truth. Consequently, man without information of the actual spiritual form of sex has accepted perverted material sex life as the all in all. (SB 1.1.1 Purport)

MISDEEDS BETRAY PRETENDERS

Oh brahmana, one's true character cannot remain hidden, no matter how hard one tries to conceal it. Misdeeds will always betray those who have not conquered the forces of lust, anger and greed. (Ramayana; Uttara-khanda; Bhakti Vikasa Swami; Lord Ramacandra speaking to Sarvatha-siddha)

330 MILLION DEMIGODS

Prabhupāda: There are 33, I mean to say, crores. One crore equal to?
Devotee: Ten million.
Prabhupāda: Ten million, and thirty-three. Just see. There are so many

demigods, and so many desires also. (Śrīmad-Bhāgavatam 2.3.1-3 — Los Angeles, May 22, 1972)

Demigod worshipers will go to the demigods. There are different planets, 33 crores of demigods, and there are thirty-three crores of planets also. (Śrīmad-Bhāgavatam 2.3.1-3 — Los Angeles, May 22, 1972)

gatvā surendra-bhavanaṁ
dattvādityai ca kuṇḍale
pūjitas tridaśendreṇa
mahendryāṇyā ca sa-priyaḥ
codito bhāryayotpāṭya
pārījātaṁ garutmati
āropya sendrān vibudhān
nirjityopānayat puram

SYNONYMS: gatvā—going; sura—of the demigods; indra—of the King; bhavanam—to the abode; dattvā—giving; adityai—to Aditi, the mother of Indra; ca—and; kuṇḍale—her earrings; pūjitaḥ—worshiped; tridaśa—of the thirty (chief demigods); indreṇa—by the chief; mahā-indryāṇyā—by the wife of Lord Indra; ca—and; sa—together with; priyaḥ—His beloved (Queen Satyabhāmā); coditaḥ—urged; bhāryayā—by His wife; utpāṭya—uprooting; pārijātam—the pārijāta tree; garutmati—on Garuḍa; āropya—placing; sa-indrān—including Indra; vibudhān—the demigods; nirjitya—defeating; upānayat—He brought; puram—to His city.

TRANSLATION: The Lord then went to the abode of Indra, the demigods' king, and gave mother Aditi her earrings; there Indra and his wife worshiped Kṛṣṇa and His beloved consort Satyabhāmā. Then, at Satyabhāmā's behest the Lord uprooted the heavenly pārijāta tree and put it on the back of Garuḍa. After defeating Indra and all the other demigods, Kṛṣṇa brought the pārijāta to His capital. (SB 10.59.40) [Editor's note: The conclusion is there are 330 million demigods, but tridasa pur means the 30 chief demigods according to Srimad Bhagavatam 10.59.40]

DEMIGOD WORSHIP

1. Sri Siva said: Now I will tell you the most confidential secret. By following this with faith one will attain firm devotion to Lord Hari.
2. Abandoning the belief that by taking shelter of the demigods, going on pilgrimages, and following varnasrama-dharma one will cross beyond all miseries, one should happily surrender to Lord Krsna's lotus feet.
3. One should say, "Sri Krsna, the Supreme Personality of

Godhead, the master of the universes, is my only shelter!" and one should be devoted to the Lord's name and to one's spiritual master.

4. O brahmana, abandoning worship of the demigods by presenting offerings to them and performing other kinds of service to them, one should, aware that He is the master of all the demigods, worship Krsna alone.
5. A householder devotee of Lord Visnu should perform his inevitable regular and occasional duties and at the same time think of Lord Krsna in his mind.
6. After one has first worshipped Lord Krsna one may worship the demigods according to the rules of scripture, but one must always remember Lord Krsna in one's heart.
7. Otherwise one should not worship the demigods and one should not follow the injunctions and prohibitions of demigod-worship.
8. For they who renounce wife, children, friends, and others, take shelter of Lord Krsna, and devotedly chant His glories, there is no other duty to be performed.
9. A person who to attain material desires worships the demigods and makes offerings to them falls down from devotional service. He does not leave this world of repeated birth and death.
10. A merciless materialist, whose heart is filled with lusty desires, and who kills an animal, is tortured in hell for years equalling the number of hairs on the animal's body.
11. There is no sin in killing animals offered in Vedic sacrifices. Still, that is the path of they who have material desires. The path of renunciation is better.
12. The lowest of men kill animals in the course of worshipping the demigods. If somehow they go to the heavenly planets, they must later also go to hell.
13. "As I eat his flesh (mamsa) now, so he (sa) in the future will eat me (mam)." In this way the wise explain the derivation of the word "mamsa" (meat).
14. They who take shelter of devotional service to Lord Visnu and then kill animals without offering them in worship to the demigods fall from the path of devotional service.
15. Living entities who attain the human form of live and do not worship Lord Hari's feet or take shelter of Him alone, attain a wretched birth as an unmoving plant or similar living entity.
16. Brahma, Indra and I worship Lord Krsna day and night. What demigod is better than Lord Krsna, the Supreme Personality of Godhead?

17. All people and their rulers yearn to attain His mercy. Even though He ignores her, goddess Laksmi serves His feet.
18. What demigod is greater than Lord Krsna, the beloved of Laksmi and the saviour from miseries? What person engaged in chanting His names does not attain the supreme abode?
19. Service to His feet is the root from which material piety, economic development, sense gratification and liberation grow. What demigod is greater than Him? He is an ocean of mercy. He has a noble heart.
20. The smallest service He considers very great. What demigod is greater than Him? He is easy to worship. He is the master of the universes.
21. Whoever somehow or other worships Him attains the perfection he desires. He attains liberation. He attains fearlessness.
22. What demigod is greater than Lord Krsna, the son of Devaki-devi? He descended to the material world to reveal His glories and liberate the people.
23. Therefore one should abandon the worship of the demigods and the presentation of offerings to them. Following the teachings of a bona-fide spiritual master, one should worship Lord Krsna's feet. (Satvata Tantra: Lord Siva to Narada Patala 8)

One should have unalloyed devotion to Lord Krsna. One should not worship the demigods thinking them independent of Lord Krsna. However, when you see other people worshipping the demigods, you should not be disrespectful to the demigods. You should honour the demigods, but always remember that all the demigods worship Lord Krsna. As long as the heart remains in the grip of the three material modes, one cannot attain unalloyed devotion to Lord Krsna. Only persons overpowered by goodness, passion, and ignorance worship the demigods with the idea that the demigods are equal to Lord Krsna. These persons are qualified only to have faith in the demigods. Therefore one should not disrespect their method of worship. By the mercy of the demigods, these persons will gradually become elevated. Eventually their hearts will become free of the three material modes. (Jaiva Dharma; Ch. 20)

NO DISCIPLES WHILE GURU ALIVE

Siddhasvarupa does not want to take disciples, neither he should have disciples while I am alive. That is the process. (Letter to: Sudevi — Los Angeles 15 September, 1972)

SINCERITY—NOT RESULTS

So we have to do our business. Let the dogs bark on. We don't care for it. If we remain sincere to Krsna, that is our victory, not the result. Karmany evadhikaras te ma phalesu kadacana. We have to act according to direction of Krsna, that much. We want to see good result. Even there is no good result, we don't mind. We must be sincere to Krsna that "We have done our best." That's all. Without cheating Krsna. That is our duty. As servant, we shall not cheat the master. Result, no result — that depends on Krsna. We should not be sorry if there is not result. Never mind. Caitanya Mahaprabhu says that "I have brought to Benares hari-nama, but here they are full of Mayavadis. So if it is not sold, all right, I shall take it back." Caitanya Mahaprabhu said. So we should not be anxious whether the things are sold or not. But we must do our best canvassing work: "Please take it." That is our duty. Hare Krsna. (Conversation on Train to Allahabad— January 11, 1977, India)

DREAM INSTRUCTIONS

Sometimes He tells His devotee in a dream that His temple and His garden are now very old and that He cannot enjoy them very nicely. Thus He requests the devotee to repair them. Sometimes He is buried in the earth, and as if unable to come out Himself, He requests His devotee to rescue Him. Sometimes He requests His devotee to preach His glories all over the world, although He alone is quite competent to perform this task. (SB 6.19.5 Purport)

58 ROUNDS A DAY

While thinking of himself as the most unfavored disciple of Prabhu, Nityananda used to address his disciples and say, "O my dear fellows, if you want to attain the feet of Krsna, you should take his name one lakh times daily." (Prema Vilasa ch. 18)

If a devotee can complete one lac Harinama's in a nama mala**, he will attain the feet of Sri Krsna.

He explained that a devotee should carefully chant his rounds, touching his mala to his forehead after completing each round. [Prema Vilasa, Ch. 11 by Nityananda dasa (disciple of Jahnavi devi) Lokanantha Goswami to Narottama dasa Thakura; Translations are by Kusakratha Prabhu.]

ITEMS OF DEVOTION

In this material world many things become dear to a person. To accept the relation that all these things have to Lord Krsna is called "offering a favourite article". (Jaiva Dharma, Ch. 20)

- observing a great festival without performing a fire-sacrifice is to be avoided (Satvata Tantra 4.28: Lord Siva Speaking)

- When the scent of flowers offered to the Lord enters the nose, the prison cage of one's past sins suddenly breaks open. (Satvata Tantra 4.28)

CHANTING

- Only with great endeavour do human beings attain success in remembering Lord Krsna. However, merely by moving their lips they can attain success in chanting the Lord's holy name. (Satvata Tantra)

INSTINCT

So although his eyes are all closed—you have seen the dogs—but because in his previous life as dog he had the experience where to find out the food, so even though it cannot see, it traces out where is the food. That is past experience and that is the proof of the continuation of the soul eternally. Just like I am living in this room and, say, for ten years I am absent from this room, but after ten years when I come here, immediately I remember where is the toilet, where is my sitting place, everything. So that remembrance comes from the last visit. So a living entity is passing through different species of form. That is his material life. So in some previous life, millions of years, when he was a dog, he knew where to find out his food, so immediately in the dog's body again, he remembers. (Srila Prabhupada: Discussions on John Locke)

PREPARED LECTURES

Yes, it is good to be prepared with a well-thought lecture in advance. However, we must be able to preach effectively at a moment's notice or under any conditions or circumstances also. As you begin to study the Sanskrit words, in each word you will find a treasure house of different understanding. (Letter to: Satsvarupa — Los Angeles 1 July, 1972)

He says, "If you throw away His grace, He punishes you by behaving objectively toward you, and in that sense one may say that the world has not got a personal God in spite of all the proofs. But while dons and parsons," that is priests, "drivel on," talk on, "about the millions of truths about God's personality, the truth is that there are no longer the men living who could bear the pressure and weight of having a personal God." Because he feels that a personal God would make demands on man, and so therefore men reject the idea of a personal God. (Soren Aabye Kierkegaard)

IMAGINARY NIRVANA

The highest stage of impersonal liberation is called 'nirvana', where the individual souls imagine that they cease to exist. However, the spirit souls exist eternally. That is their nature. Therefore this imaginary 'nirvana' never actually occurs.(Jaiva Dharma: Ch.12, P.10)

A soul averse to Lord Krsna, is bound by Lord Krsna's shadow-potency maya, who binds that soul with ropes of goodness, passion and ignorance. (Jaiva Dharma; CH.7 P.7)

INTERFAITH

There is only one religion. There is no such thing as two religions. That one religion is called "the eternal religion" or "the Vaisnava religion". Other religions are temporary. They serve as steps leading up to the Vaisnava religions. (Jaiva Dharma; p89)

HOW WE FELL?

It was by accident that the individual soul first fell into the cycle of karma. What was that chance accident? The followers of karma-mimamsa claim that karma has no beginning, but the truth is that there is a root from which karma has grown. In the individual soul's aversion to the Supreme Personality of Godhead is the accident that is the root of karma. As that is believed to be an accident, so eternal pious deeds may also be believed to be chance accidents. (Jaiva Dharma P.82)

MECHANICAL SERVICE?

Giving charity and performing yoga, when connected to devotional service, are activities that lead to devotional service. In the scriptures it is said that cleaning the temple of Lord Hari, offering a lamp to tulasi-devi, fasting on ekadasi and other like activities, are activities of devotional service. Even if they are performed without pure faith, or even if they are performed accidentally, these pious activities still increase one's devotion for the Lord. When these pious deeds gradually become powerful, after many births they lead to pure faith in the association of devotees and the performance of pure devotional service. (Jaiva Dharma, P.82)

MEAT-EATER MEANS MEATHEAD

Prabhupāda: Parīkṣit Mahārāja. He said that God consciousness, Kṛṣṇa consciousness, cannot be understood by the animal killer. Vinā paśughnāt [SB 10.1.4]. Nivṛtta-tarṣair upagīyamānāt. You'll find those who are animal killers, the so-called Christians and Mohammedans, they cannot understand. They (are) simply fanatics. Cannot understand what is soul, what is God. They have got some theories and they are thinking we are religionists. What is sin, what is pious activities, these things are not understood by them because they are animal killers. It is not possible. Therefore Lord Buddha propagated ahiṁsā. Ahiṁsā. Because he saw the whole human race is going to hell by this animal killing. "Let me stop them so that they may, in future, they may become sober." Sadaya-hṛdaya darśita: Two sides. First of all he was very much compassionate, that poor animals, they are being killed. And another side, he saw "The whole human race is going to hell. So let me do something." Therefore he had to deny the existence of the soul because their brain will not tolerate such things. Therefore he did not say anything about the soul or God. He said that "You stop animal killing." If I pinch you, you feel pain. So why should you give pain to others? Never mind he has no soul; that's all right. He did not talk anything about soul. So these people say the animals have no soul. But that's all right, but he's feeling pain when you are killing the animal. So you also feel pain. So why should you give pain to others? That is Lord Buddha's theory. Sadaya-hṛdaya darśita-paśu-ghātam. (Lecture: Bhagavad-gītā 2.18 — London, August 24, 1973)

WHY YUDHISTHIRA SAW HELL

Some people think that Yudhisthira Maharaja was obliged to see hell because he told a lie, i.e. he said that Asvatthama was slain in the presence of Dronacarya. Yet Srila Prabhupada gives a different reason for his seeing hell:

So Kṛṣṇa asked Mahārāja Yudhiṣṭhira that "You go because you are recognized truthful, dharmarāja. So when you will say, this is also false, he will believe." But Yudhiṣṭhira hesitated, "How can I tell lie?" He disobeyed the order of Kṛṣṇa, and he wanted to become very truthful. For this reason he had to see hell. (Bhagavad-gītā 1.45-46 — London, August 1, 1973)

So those who are mundane moralist, they cannot understand this thing, because they are mundane platform. The another example is that Yudhiṣṭhira Mahārāja. He was asked by Kṛṣṇa that "You speak lie to Dronācārya that 'Your son is dead.' " Yudhiṣṭhira Mahārāja refused. For this he had to see hell. He was more moralist than Kṛṣṇa. For this moral activity he had to visit hell. (Room Conversation — May 5, 1976, Honolulu)

LIBERALISM AND THE CATHOLIC CHURCH

This is a quote from a book by Judge Robert Bork, whose words below are of relevance for ISKCON today. (Submitted by His Holiness Bhakti Vikasa Swami)

"Radical egalitarianism and individualism have altered much in American life. The question of just how irresistible they are, the test case of whether any institution can maintain its integrity in the face of the deforming pressures of a modern liberal culture is, of course, the Roman Catholic Church. What is to be seen is whether the church can maintain its doctrines and its institutional structure in the face of pressure both from without and from within.

"The Roman Catholic Church is the test case because, as Hitchcock put it, 'few religions in the history of the world have placed more emphasis on doctrinal purity, liturgical correctness, and moral authenticity than has the Catholic Church. . . . If at almost all times in the history of the church, a concern for orthodoxy has been paramount, the contemporary Church has an eerie feel about it precisely because of the absence of that concern.' If, despite powerful and orthodox American bishops, orthodoxy is no longer a major concern in the American church, that is surely a sign that the church is giving way to the culture. The church's opposition to abortion, homosexual conduct, and the ordination of women is under attack and appears to be a minority position among the Catholic laity, perhaps even among the American bishops. If the church gives way on any of those issues, the culture will have effectively destroyed it. The other reason the church arouses hostility is that its structure is hierarchical and authoritative, in addition to the fact that its priesthood is male. It has clear lines of authority of the pope. These are matters that create no small outrage in the egalitarians of our time, and one sees even within the church demands that it be democratized, that it accept beliefs and behavior it has always condemned, and that it accept radical alterations of its ancient structure. Columnists pronounce the church out of touch with the people in the pews and find that reason for the church to change.

"That is not reason for the church to change. The protestant mainline denominations are out of touch with the people in the pews because the churches' leadership changed, moving well to the left of their membership. That is a different situation than a church that is trying to remain unchanged while the culture changes its members. If the church changes doctrine and structure to follow its members' views, it is difficult to see the value of that church and its religion. Religions must claim to be true and, in their essentials, to uphold principles that are universal and eternal. No church that panders to the zeitgeist deserves respect, except from those who find it politically useful, and that is less respect than disguised contempt." (from "Slouching Toward Gomorrah" by Robert Bork.)

IF YOU COMPROMISE—THEN NOBODY WILL CARE

Prabhupāda: Now who knew that in Europe and America or all over the world, Hare Kṛṣṇa will go on? Bon Mahārāja left the field; others left the field. You see? Other swamis came. They talked all nonsense, yoga, this and that, nose pressing, eyes pressing—all finished. Now Hare Kṛṣṇa is going on. Now people, the nose-presser and eyes-presser, they are no more important. Is it not? Eh? Now our men go and challenge these rascals. And in New York they did it, huh?

Devotee: Yes.

Prabhupāda: And they are afraid of our troops. (laughter) They are afraid.

Madhudviṣa: One of those nose-pressers, he once was speaking, and he said, "These Hare Kṛṣṇa people, they like me very much. They always come to my lectures and they sell all the books, all their books, and then they go away before I start to talk."

Prabhupāda: "You go on pressing your nose. We make our business and go away." (laughter)

Madhudviṣa: He was speaking like that because our men go into the lecture dressed in disguise, plain clothes, and we are going in the audience selling books to everyone. They all get the book, and then, when he begins to speak, then we all turn around and go out.

Prabhupāda: Yes, they did it in the Guru Maharaji's camp also. Hundreds of Bhagavad-gītā As It Is sold.

Satsvarūpa: Thousands.

Prabhupāda: Thousands. So we take advantage of this meeting. We do our business and go away. And they have no books. They have simply that pressing of nose, that's all, nothing else. They have no philosophy, nothing of the sort. What they will write? They have no philosophy. Simply cheat that "Press your nose; you get Bhagavān." That's all. And people think, "It is so easy. Why shall I go to Bhaktivedanta Swami? Let me go to this Guru Mahārāja." They think like that. And some of our men, feeling too much pressure, they go away. But here there is nothing cheap, that simply by pressing nose and eyes and you become God. Don't make compromise. This principle must be observed. Then you'll remain strong. As soon as you make compromise, then it is finished. Dṛḍha-vratāḥ. Find out this verse. Dṛḍha-vratāḥ. What is that? Bhajante māṁ dṛḍha-vratāḥ. Namasyantaś ca māṁ...

Cāru: Bhajante māṁ dṛḍha-vratāḥ.

Prabhupāda: Ah, ah. That dṛḍha-vratāḥ must be there, strong determination. Then it will go on. The scientists will come to learn and the psychiatrists will come to learn if you keep dṛḍha-vratāḥ. And as soon as you make compromise, then nobody will care for. (Room Conversation with Devotees — July 2, 1974, Melbourne)

QUESTIONS AND ANSWERS

"INTERFAITH DIALOGUE"

QUESTION: How should I regard the other religions in the various countries of the world?

ANSWER: (By Srila Bhaktivinoda Thakura) Religion is one. It is not two, and it is not many. There is only one religion for the soul. That religion is called the Vaisnava religion. There is no reason why religion should be different from different languages, countries and peoples. The religion of the soul may be called by different names, but it is not possible that there can be different religions. The religion of the soul is the pure love the atomic spiritual entity bears for the supreme spiritual entity. Because of differing material conceptions, some spirit souls have distorted that original religion and given it a variety of different shapes. The pure and original form of the soul's religion is the Vaisnava religion. Other so-called religions are merely distorted forms of the Vaisnava religion. Other religions are pure to the degree that they are like the Vaisnava religion.

"SOUL'S FALL"

QUESTION: How is it that a soul can fall down from the spiritual world?

ANSWER: (By Srila Bhaktivinoda Thakura) The individual soul is spiritual. Nevertheless the spiritual soul may be placed under the control of inanimate matter.

Thus the individual soul is not like the spiritual world, which never comes into contact with the material world. Nor is the individual soul like inanimate matter. In this sense the individual soul is neither spirit nor matter. That is why it is true that the Supreme Personality of Godhead and the individual spirit souls are different beings eternally. (Jaiva Dharma Chapter 1; Page 11)

"IMMOVABLE"

QUESTION: In Bhagavad-gītā, it says that the soul is immovable. In the Second Chapter there is a verse that says the soul is immovable. What does that mean exactly? Are we not moving?

ANSWER: (By Srila Prabhupada) Sometimes, because of mental derangement, the land appears to be moving. A drunkard, for example, or a person with heart disease, sometimes feels that the land is moving. Similarly, the reflections of trees in a flowing river also appear to move. These are the actions of māyā. Actually the living entity does not move (sthāṇur acalo 'yam). The living entity does not take birth or accept death, but because of the transient subtle and gross bodies, the living entity appears to move from one place to another or be dead and gone forever. As the great Bengali Vaiṣṇava poet, Jagadānanda Paṇḍita, has said:

piśācī pāile yena mati-cchanna haya
māyā-grasta jīvera haya se bhāva udaya

According to this statement from the Prema-vivarta, when a living entity is conditioned by material nature, he is exactly like a person haunted by a ghost. One should therefore understand the fixed position of the spirit soul and how he is carried away by the waves of material nature to different bodies and different situations under lamentation and hankering. One achieves the success of life when he understands the constitutional position of his self and is undisturbed by the conditions created by material nature (prakṛteḥ kriyamāṇāni guṇaiḥ karmāṇi sarvaśaḥ). (SB 7.2.23 Purport)

"WORLD WAR III"

QUESTION: How should devotees prepare for World War III?

ANSWER: (By Srila Prabhupada) Haṁsadūta: So Prabhupāda, is there something we should do to prepare ourselves for this disaster?
Prabhupāda: What?
Haṁsadūta: This coming war.
Prabhupāda: You should simply prepare for chanting Hare Kṛṣṇa.
Haṁsadūta: That's all?
Prabhupāda: That's all. (Morning Walk Conversation (World War III) — April 4, 1975, Māyāpur)

"EDUCATIONAL TRAINING FOR NEW DEVOTEES"

QUESTION: Could you comment on what may be seen as a problematic kind of elite atmosphere which is created around educational and training programs, either willingly or unknowingly.

ANSWER: (By Danavir Goswami) Regarding your question about training and education; in my experience people join our movement not to work. They join primarily to find happiness, knowledge and relief from distress. Most Westerners do not need economic help, they need spiritual training. However they realize that they need to do something to keep busy and to help the organization as well as to please the Lord, guru and devotees so they agree to perform devotional service.

That service has to be carefully regulated otherwise it begins to seem like mundane work especially for newcomers. I've found that six hours is about as much as a devotee really wants to work or do service. The rest of the time he wants to chant (kirtan, japa, aratis), hear and give classes, study, discuss with other devotees, take prasadam, etc. Engaging new devotees requires careful attention. Idle time is dangerous too.

Later a devotee wants to work more, but in my opinion, he should be careful about doing that because he needs to balance his spiritual life. Too much work can be risky. Ramesvara was really a hard worker—from 4 am to 10 pm every day he was engaged, primarily in his BBT services. He neglected his rounds though and it snuffed out his advancement. Bhagavan was a brilliant devotee but he neglected study and writing (which Srila Prabhupada told him to do) and he fell victim to women. Harikesa put his management ahead of sadhana and look what happened. Healthy balance is required—sadhana and services.

If new devotees learn how to be regulated and fully engaged they have a better chance of becoming solid devotees. Fully engaged doesn't mean ten hours of pot washing or ten hours of book distribution or emergencies all the time. Up to six hours of intensive service is good but that also should be in proper association, environment and guidance otherwise that also will become mundane for them.

They want enlightenment, realizations, mercy, bliss, nectar, transcendental knowledge and therefore they need enough activities which concentrate on these things. Morning and evening programs, classes, kirtans, counseling, etc. Of course running restaurants are not so compatible for these things that is why that service is mostly meant for householders who have another impetus—money, family, home, etc.

I have explained these things to help you understand why new devotees will naturally be attracted to bhakta programs or other well-organized programs of learning and spiritually-stimulating activities. The initial investment of time and energy put into training new devotees however pays off in greater profits as the new devotees become happily situated in Krishna consciousness for life.

"BHAGAVAT SAPTAHA"

QUESTION: It is widely documented that Srila Prabhupada spoke disparagingly about the well-known social convention of holding Bhagavat Saptaha (seven day) recitals of Srimad Bhagavatam. He said they were not bona fide and not endorsed by any Gaudiya acaryas.

However, did he ever encourage ISKCON devotees to use the popularity of the Bhagavat Saptaha format, i.e. holding a special seven day recital of Srimad Bhagavatam?

ANSWER: (By His Grace Yasomatinandana dasa Adhikari) It happened like this. One day I asked Shrila Prabhupada in Bombay, what did he think about Dongre Maharaja, the most famous Bhagavat saptah speaker in India.

I said he cries while speaking and makes the public also cry. Srila Prabhupada said I don't know. What does he say? I said even though he glorifies Krsna, he also says one should chant the mantra for whoever is his ishtadeva. In other words, Lord Shiva's devotee should chant Om namah Shivaya and mother Durga's or Ganesha devotee should chant their mantras.

So Srila Prabhupada laughed and said," That means he is not Dongre. He is Dhongare (Dhonga means pretender). I said he is a good speaker so he bewilders the masses. Then Srila Prabhupada said, "so why don't you speak?" I was little puzzled because I always heard and read that Srila Prabhupada was against Saptaha, so I said "Bhagavat saptaha?" He said," Yes. if people want to hear saptaha, we can tell them the right thing. He is misleading them, so you speak and tell them the right philosophy."

That is one thing I should have started long time ago as it was directly told to me by Srila Prabhupada. But I always felt the speaker should be free from material desires. So I always felt unqualified to do so. On the other hand, if I speak like a postman and simply repeat from Srila Prabhupada's books, I should be OK. Some of my friends like Shridhar Maharaja has been pushing me to do so. I hope one of these days I will gather enough energy to do that.

I don't think Srila Prabhupada gave a blanket endorsement for Bhagavat Saptaha by the above conversation, but as usual he was pragmatic. Preaching is the essence and utility is the principle. I do agree that it shouldn't be an "OK" or "in" thing for ISKCON devotees but if one can preach and attract outsiders in the name of Bhagavat saptaha, it can be done. Then again who is to judge? So it would be hard to legislate. An individual temple can form its policy based on discrimination, which is the better part of valour.

When Srila Prabhupada speaks against the Saptaha hearing he is speaking against the idea of ritualistic hearing. Some people think that simply by mechanically sitting in a Bhagavat saptaha as a ritual, one can be liberated. Another point is that the speaker tries to fly over the topics to cover the whole Bhagavatam in seven days. Sometimes the speaker doesn't even touch the original Bhagavatam but simply tells his own version of the stories in a palatable way. Obviously Srila Prabhupada was against such professional saptaha reciters. That is all wrong. Since ninety nine percent saptaha reciters are professional speakers, Srila Prabhupada condemns the whole idea, otherwise how can it be wrong to preach the right philosophy either for 7 minutes or seven days or one hour or seven hours? Any preaching for any time limit is auspicious if it is bonafide.

"VINEGAR"

QUESTION: A question has arisen amongst devotees regarding vinegar. We have found one quote from Srila Prabhupada in the folio as follows: "So far the cucumber pickles: As far as possible we should not offer to the Deity things which are prepared by nondevotees. We can accept from them raw fruits, grains or similar raw things. So far cooking and preparing, that should be strictly limited to the initiated devotees. And aside from this, vinegar is not good; it is tamasic, in the darkness, nasty food. So I think we shall not accept this pickles." (March 24, 1969 Letters)

ANSWER: (By Danavir Goswami) I have not heard of Srila Prabhupada eating foods with vinegar in them. Nevertheless, I do not see how one could justify offering anything with vinegar in it to the temple deity since Srila Prabhupada plainly said it was not good and also because vinegar contains alcohol. The tongue is voracious and urges the soul to put aside good or transcendental prudence in favor of immediate gratification.

"A TEST FOR SPIRITUAL ADVANCEMENT"

QUESTION: How can one test if he or she is making spiritual advancement?

ANSWER: (By Srila Prabhupada) So the test is within our hand. If during maṅgala-ārati we feel laziness, that means I'm not yet spiritually advanced. And if one feels enthused, "Now it is time for maṅgala-ārati, let me stand up, let me do this," then it is spiritual. Anyone can test. Bhaktiḥ pareśānubhavo viraktir anyatra syāt. (Lecture; London, August 26, 1973)

VRNDAVANA TALKS

Danavir Goswami addresses topics which he discussed in Vrndavana 2001.

UDDHAVA

You said that Uddhava, Lord Krishna's cousin-brother and dear friend, was a jnana-misra-bhakta[1]. This term, jnana-misra-bhakta refers to one who performs devotional service with the desire for liberation by merging into the Brahman effulgence[2]. Such a person's bhakti is adulterated with impersonal jnana and he is not a pure devotee[3]. This type of jnana whereby the philosopher concludes that he is one with the brahman is different from the jnana whereby a pure devotee loves the Lord while recognizing Him (jnana) to have the opulence (aisvarya) of the Supreme Personality of Godhead. The jnana of the pure devotees who reside in Dvaraka and Mathura is not the same as the jnana of the mixed devotee/impersonalist neophyte jnana-misra bhaktas.

Uddhava's pure, unadulterated and spontaneous love for Krishna is unquestionable, therefore to refer to him as a jnana-misra-bhakta is, in our opinion, not only inaccurate but insulting. At the end of the class you gave, I asked where you received this information that Uddhava was a jnana-misra-bhakta; you replied that it was from a Hindi movie you had seen—not a good source from which to minimize the Lord's greatest devotee.

It is true that Sri Uddhava was deputed to Vrndavana to solace the Vrijbasis and to deliver Lord Krishna's own message to the gopis. It was Lord Krishna's own words in His own letter, however, which contained instructions on analytical knowledge. It is also true that Sri Uddhava was a recognized scholar and disciple of the greatly learned priest of the demigods, Brhaspati. Certainly Uddhava had studied and understood the Upanisadic Vedic texts espousing knowledge of brahman.

The great devotee Uddhava once wrote a letter to Krsna, "My dear Krsna, I have just finished the study of all kinds of philosophical books and Vedic verses about the goal of life, and so now I have a little reputation for my studies. But still, in spite of my reputation, my knowledge is condemned, because although enjoying the effulgence of Vedic knowledge, I could not appreciate the effulgence emanating from the nails of Your toes. Therefore, the sooner my pride and Vedic knowledge are finished, the better it will be!" (Nectar of Devotion 38: Indifference and Separation)

Yet despite Uddhava's qualifications as a brilliant Vedic scholar, he is also revered by the Srimad Bhagavatam and Vaisnava acaryas as a nitya-siddha pure devotee of Lord Krishna[4].

yah panca-hayano matra
pratar-asaya yacitah
tan naicchad racayan yasya
saparyam bala-iilaya

He was one who even in his childhood, at the age of five years, was so absorbed in the service of Lord Krsna that when he was called by his mother for morning breakfast, he did not wish to have it.

PURPORT: From his very birth, Uddhava was a natural devotee of Lord Krsna, or a nitya-siddha, a liberated soul. From natural instinct he used to serve Lord Krsna, even in his childhood. He used to play with dolls in the form of Krsna, he would serve the dolls by dressing, feeding and worshiping them, and thus he was constantly absorbed in the play of transcendental realization. These are the signs of an eternally liberated soul.

Srila Prabhupada specifically explains that Uddhava, unlike Maitreya, was not a mixed devotee (jnana-bhakta) but a spotlessly pure devotee.

Although both Uddhava and Maitreya were great souls, the Lord's attention was more on Uddhava because he was a spotlessly pure devotee. A jnana bhakta, or one whose devotion is mixed with the monistic viewpoint, is not a pure devotee. Although Maitreya was a devotee, his devotion was mixed. (Srimad Bhagavatam 3.4.10 Purport)

Lord Sri Caitanya Mahaprabhu verified, "On the surface of the world there is no devotee greater than Uddhava. Uddhava desires to take on his head the dust of the gopis' lotus feet.[5]" Wishing to corroborate the unparalleled postion of the gopis, Lord Krishna sent the great sage Uddhava to Vrndavana and as a result Uddhava established for all time that the gopis' love for Krishna is supreme:

"My dear gopis, the mentality you have developed in relationship with Krsna is very, very difficult to attain, even for great sages and saintly persons. You have attained the highest perfectional stage of life. It is a great boon for you that you have fixed your minds upon Krsna and have decided to have Krsna only, giving up your families, homes, relatives, husbands and children for the sake of the Supreme Personality. Because your minds are now fully absorbed in Krsna, the Supreme Soul, universal love has automatically developed in you. I think myself very fortunate that I have been favored, by your grace, to see you in this situation." (Spoken by Sri Uddhava: Krishna Book 47: Delivery of the Message of Krsna to the Gopis)

Srila Rupa Goswami richly describes Uddhava's ecstatic symptoms of love for Krishna in Bhakti Rasamrta Sindhu[6].

There is a statement about Uddhava's symptoms of love. When he saw Lord Kṛṣṇa his eyes filled with tears and created a river which flowed down toward the sea of Kṛṣṇa to offer tribute, as a wife offers tribute to her husband. When his body erupted with goose pimples, he appeared like the kadamba flower, and when he began to offer prayers, he appeared completely distinct from all other devotees. (Nectar of Devotion Chapter 37: Impetuses for Kṛṣṇa's Service)

Sri Uddhava knew well that Lord Krishna is the Supreme Personality of Godhead and was likely the most qualified person to establish the fact after the departure of the Lord from this earth. As a resident of Dvaraka and a devotee in reverential friendship,[7] Uddhava's emotions are indeed distinct from the non-reverential devotion of the residents of Vrndavana. In Vrndavana the friends of Krishna climb on His shoulders or play jokes on Him—both actions would be unthinkable for Uddhava. (Brihad Bhagavatamrta)

He was a great devotee, Uddhava. He was more advanced than Arjuna. There are different grades of devotees. The first-class devotees were the gopis, the damsels of Vrndavana. Nobody could be compared with their devotional service. So next were Uddhava, then Arjuna. (Lecture by Srila Prabhupada; Sri Caitanya-caritamrta, Madhya-lila 20.137-142 — New York, November 29, 1966)

Persons wishing to define Uddhava's love as subordinate to the level of the Vrijavasis may do so and that is acceptable. However, Lord Krishna

Himself states that Uddhava is more dear to Him than even the Goddess of Fortune:

My dear Uddhava, neither Lord Brahma, Lord Siva, Lord Sankarsana, the goddess of fortune nor indeed My own self are as dear to Me as you are. (Srimad Bhagavatam 11.14.15)

Uddhava's pure, unadulterated and spontaneous love for Krishna is unquestionable[8], therefore to refer to him as a jñāna-miśra-bhakta is, in our opinion, not only inaccurate but insulting.

Footnotes:

1. Srila Visvanatha Cakravarti Thakura describes that this impersonal feature, or Brahman manifestation, of the Supreme Lord is meant for persons who are essentially very advanced but still not able to understand the personal features or variegatedness of the spiritual world. Such devotees are known as jnana-misra-bhaktas, or devotees whose devotional service is mixed with empiric knowledge. (Srimad Bhagavatam 4.9.16 Purport)

2. Srimad Bhagavatam 10.10.20-22 (Purport)

3. Lecture by Srila Prabhupada on Srimad-Bhagavatam 1.1.3 — Caracas, February 24, 1975

4. (Srimad Bhagavatam 3.2.2 and Purport)

5. pradhana prthivite bhakta nahi uddhava-samana... tenha yanra pada-dhuli karena prarthana

Caitanya Caritamrta Antya 7.46-7

6. (Nectar of Devotion 37: Impetuses for Krsna's Service)

7. Nectar of Devotion 32; Pure and Mixed Flavors

8. The Srimad Bhagavatam 3.2.5-6 & Purports confirm Uddhava's position:

"It was so observed by Vidura that Uddhava had all the transcendental bodily changes due to total ecstasy, and he was trying to wipe away tears of separation from his eyes. Thus Vidura could understand that Uddhava had completely assimilated extensive love for the Lord. The great devotee Uddhava soon came back from the abode of the Lord to the human plane, and wiping his eyes, he awakened his reminiscence of the past and spoke to Vidura in a pleasing mood."

PURPORTS: The symptoms of the highest order of devotional life were observed by Vidura, an experienced devotee of the Lord, and he confirmed Uddhava's perfectional stage of love of Godhead. Ecstatic bodily changes are manifested from the spiritual plane and are not artificial expressions developed by practice...

In the Bhakti-rasamrta-sindhu by Srila Rupa Gosvami, the chief disciple of Lord Sri Caitanya Mahaprabhu, these transcendental symptoms displayed by pure devotees like Uddhava are systematically described...When Uddhava was fully absorbed in the transcendental ecstasy of love of God, he actually forgot all about the external world...When Uddhava wanted to speak to Vidura, he came down from the abode of the Lord, Dvaraka, to the material plane of human beings. ...That Uddhava attained this stage is evident from his dealings. He could simultaneously reach the supreme planet and still appear in this world.

DRY SADHANA

You described the performance of sadhana bhakti as "dry." While your intent was to contrast dry sadhana with juicy prema which is not necessarily incorrect or correct, the effect of your statement deprecated sadhana bhakti. However such deprecation is not in line with the method Srila Prabhupada and Rupa Goswami taught. They taught that one should enthusiastically engage in sadhana bhakti (utsaha) and naturally that service will become spontaneous and enriched with higher realizations and love. Not that one should try to polevault over sadhana into prema, siddha deha, siddha pranali, siddha swarupa, etc. Looking around Vrndavana we see many Westerners doing just that— becoming entangled in so many concocted and unbonafide attempts at prema neglecting the proper system of sadhana bhakti thinking it fallaciously to be dry.

Furthermore it is incorrect to say that sadhana bhakti is dry if it is properly performed.

"The complete functional activities of a pure devotee are always engaged in the service of the Lord, and thus the pure devotees exchange feelings of ecstasy between themselves and relish transcendental bliss. This transcendental bliss is experienced even in the stage of devotional practice (sadhana-avastha), if properly undertaken under the guidance of a bona fide spiritual master." (SB 2.3.12 Purport)

The term "dry" is used for mental speculation not devotional service in practice.

"According to Srila Visvanatha Cakravarti Thakura, the path of bhakti-yoga is so joyful and practical that even in the stage of sadhana-bhakti, in which one follows rules and regulations without an advanced understanding, one can perceive the ultimate result. As stated by Srila Rupa Gosvami (Bhakti-rasamrta-sindhu 1.2.187),

iha yasya harer dasye
karmana manasa gira
nikhilasv apy avasthasu
jivan-muktah sa ucyate

As soon as one surrenders to the Supreme Lord, Krsna (prapadyamanasya), giving up all other activities (viraktir anyatra ca), one is immediately to be considered a liberated soul (jivan-muktah). The Supreme Lord, Krsna, is so merciful that when a living entity understands that the personality Krsna is the source of everything and surrenders to the Lord,

Krsna personally takes charge of him and reveals to him within his heart that he is under the Lord's full protection. Thus devotion, direct experience of the Personality of Godhead, and detachment from other objects become manifest even in the beginning stage of bhakti-yoga, since bhakti-yoga begins at the point of liberation."(SB 11.2.42 Purport)

NO GURUS FOR BRIJBASIS

You mentioned was that present-day Brijbasis require no guru and that Krishna is their guru. Perhaps you were referring to a passage in Lokanatha Swami's recent book "Festivals" as follows:

"Prabhupada went on to explain the position of Vrajavasis: "Generally Vrajavasis are naturally Krsna conscious; otherwise, how is this simple farmer offering pranamas? Even without a spiritual master they are already elevated to Krsna consciousness, because the spiritual master is within—caitya-guru. Simply by living here, if they do not commit any sin, they'll go back home, back to Godhead. "I recalled aloud Prabhupada having once said that Krsna acts like their spiritual master. To this, Prabhupada simply responded, "Krsna-guru-krpa." I understood this to mean tht the Vrajavasis have the mercy, or krpa, of Krsna, who Himself acts as their guru." (Festivals p. 197 Lokanatha Swami)

Here is the conversation as recorded and included in the Bhaktivedanta Folio:

"Lokanatha: Srila Prabhupada, what is the position of vrajavasis, those who are living in Vrndavana now? What happens to them next life?

Prabhupada: Yes. Simply by living, if they do not commit any sinful, they'll go back to home. Simply by living. Without committing any sinful activities. Always remember Krsna, this is Krsna's land, man-mana bhava mad-bhakto. That will deliver them.

Madhudvisa: They don't need a spiritual master?

Prabhupada: Yes. Spiritual master is always needed. Chadiya vaisnava-seva nistara payeche keba. Without abiding by the orders of spiritual master and serving him, nobody can be. Otherwise rascal. He has accepted one rascal spiritual master, and he cannot understand what is God, nine years, because he did not accept spiritual master.

Hari-sauri: So all these local vrajavasis, they all accept...

Prabhupada: No, vrajavasis, they are... Generally, naturally, they are Krsna conscious. Otherwise how is this illiterate farmer, he is offering? This is natural.

Pancadravida: But he has no spiritual master.

Prabhupada: Eh?

Pancadravida: He has a spiritual master?

Prabhupada: No, no, he has a spiritual master, yes. And even without spiritual master they have already elevated to Krsna consciousness.

Pancadravida: So they will go back home?

Prabhupada: Oh, yes, because spiritual master is within, caitya-guru.

Lokanatha: You said one time Krsna is there.

Prabhupada: Mm. Krsna-guru-krpa. (Morning Walk — April 9, 1976, Vrndavana)

The first key point which was not mentioned in your statement was; "Without committing any sinful activities. Always remember Krsna, this is Krsna's land, man-mana bhava mad-bhakto. That will deliver them." In your statement, since there was no qualifying explanation, the impression one received was that any Vrajavasi requires no guru even if he is sinful.

The second point is: "Spiritual master is always needed. Chadiya vaisnava-seva nistara payeche keba. Without abiding by the orders of spiritual master and serving him, nobody can be." Srila Prabhupada did not agree that one does not require a guru. He did concede that generally and naturally a person living in Vrndavana should become Krishna conscious. But that is not guaranteed. We know there are many persons living in Vrndavana engaged in nonsense, sinful activities. We know from other talks that a person living in Vrndavana who commits sinful activities must take his next birth a an animal in the dhama.

Making such a broad, unqualified statement as "Brijbasis require no guru and that Krishna is their guru" may have been an appropriate statement describing the residents of Vrndavana when Lord Krishna was present but not for today. If someone simply moves into the precincts of Vrndavana and does all nonsense does that mean he is a disciple of Krishna directly. If that were the case, why would Srila Rupa Goswami, a resident of Vrndavana, so strongly emphasize the necessity of accepting a bona fide spiritual master (and he didn't mean Krishna) in the very beginning, adau gurvasraya. All the great devotees from the time of the Six Goswamis onward who lived in Vrndavana accepted a spiritual master other than Krishna and followed his instructions scrupulously.

If one needs no guru in Vrndavana why would Srila Prabhupada bother to instruction his disciples not to hear from cheaters in Vrndavana?

For a transcendental, blissful life, chant the Hare Krsna mantra, come worship the holy place of Vrndavana, and always engage in the service of the Lord, of the spiritual master and of the Vaisnavas. This Krsna consciousness movement is therefore very safe and easy. We have only to execute the order of the Lord and fully surrender unto Him. We have only to execute the order of the spiritual master, preach Krsna consciousness and follow in the path of the Vaisnavas. (SB 4.23.7 purport)

"So you should be very, very careful. Don't go to hear any Mayavadi. There are many Mayavadis in the dress of Vaisnavas. Sri Bhaktivinoda Thakura has explained about them, that ei 'ta eka kali-cela nake tilaka gale mala, that "Here is a follower of Kali. Although he has got a tilaka on the nose and neck beads, but he's a kali-cela." If he's Mayavadi, sahaja-bhajana kache mama sange laya pare bala. So these things are there. You have come to Vrndavana. Be careful, very careful. Mayavadi-bhasya sunile. There are many Mayavadis here, many so-called tilaka-mala, but you do not know what is there inside. But great acaryas, they can find out. (Lecture: Srimad-Bhagavatam 1.7.8 — Vrndavana, September 7, 1976)

Prabhupada: The babajis, they are against anything preaching. They are very, very much against preaching. So I am preaching. Babajis, the Mayavadi sannyasis, and all of them, their idea is that I am ruining this bhajana and Hindu dharma. This is the propaganda. What I am writing, they are all wrong. And they are making... And they try to poison my disciples as far as possible so that the whole institution may be poisoned and break. This is their propaganda.

Hari-sauri: That was one thing that Nitai put in his letter, that the teachings of ISKCON are completely opposite or contradictory to what is actually in the sastra.

Prabhupada: Now he has become tiger. He wants to kill that philosophy. When he did not know anything he came to us. Now he has become learned, he wants to criticize. The same philosophy. "You have made me tiger, now I can see you are my eatable." (laughs) He could not find out any other eatable. "I shall eat you." The rascal. What can be done? (Room Conversation — October 31, 1976, Vrndavana)

If you work hard, Laksmi will come. Our institution is working so hard, all our devotees. Therefore we have no scarcity. We are not babajis, taking a mala and smoking bidi. "I do not go beyond Vrndavana." Rascal, loitering and associating with so many women, and they have become puffed-up, paramahamsas, Rupa Gosvami, imitation Rupa Gosvami. Only a loincloth of Rupa Gosvami. No education, no book writing, no going out of Vrndavana, begging. And therefore government's capturing them and giving this injection. What is that? Sterilization. Yes, just see. So many illegal children are born by these women. Bhajana. Bhajana kara. One babaji has at least three women, four women. That's all.

Hari-sauri: Like monkeys.

Prabhupada: Like monkeys, yes. Markata-vairagya. (Morning Walk — January 24, 1977, Bhubaneswar)

This Krsna consciousness movement is that para upakara. They do not know what is civilization. Such broader idea of Caitanya Mahaprabhu. He never said that "Sit down in Vrndavana and become a babaji." Kara para upakara. That is sankirtana. (Morning Walk — January 24, 1977, Bhubaneswar)

Prabhupada: So the cheaters are there. If our men are cheated, if they agree to be cheated, how can I stop them? In Vrndavana also they have done like that, the babajis.

Tamala Krsna: Same way.

Prabhupada: Nitai is victim.

Tamala Krsna: Radha-kunda. And in Vrndavana also. That Jagannatha dasa was telling you, remember, how he met some babaji coming on the road.

Prabhupada: So there are cheaters, and if one wants to be cheated, how we can stop?...

Tamala Krsna: Yeah. Jagannatha, when he was telling us about this babaji, he said that there's also these babajis, they claim to be a guru for giving initiation into their svarupa.

Prabhupada: Svarupa-siddhi.

Tamala Krsna: Yeah, svarupa-siddhi. So we can mention this as also rascaldom.

Prabhupada: Yes. What can be done? Cheaters there are. If you want to be cheated, who can save you? He has made guru without asking his guru. He submits to others. Then how we can save him?

Tamala Krsna: What does that do to his relationship with his own spiritual master?

Prabhupada: Eh?

Tamala Krsna: How does this affect his relationship with his...?

Prabhupada: They don't care for his own spiritual master.

Tamala Krsna: But what...? That means their relationship is spoiled.

Prabhupada: Yes. Guror avajna, aparadha.

Tamala Krsna: Aparadha.

Prabhupada: And Caitanya Mahaprabhu has advised, "Save yourself from aparadha." Some aparadha, and they are going away, just like Nitai. Guror avajna...

Tamala Krsna: What about this svarupa-siddhi?

Prabhupada: Svarupa-siddhi, that is bogus. Svarupa-siddhi is not that you do all nonsense things and svarupa-siddhi... Svarupa-siddhi means when he is actually liberated, he understands what is his relationship with Krsna. That is svarupa-siddhi. Sakhya... So that is far away. Unless... If he's such a fool, then where is svarupa-siddhi?

Tamala Krsna: So that realization doesn't come by some initiation from some babaji.

Prabhupada: That automatically comes when there..., he is liberated, not before. So the babajis give this mantra for svarupa-siddhi?

Tamala Krsna: Hm.

Prabhupada: Yes, this is going on...The Vrndavana also they do. These things are there, their business. And they smoke gan..., opium, ganja. Pan they are chewing, fish. "Tirtha-guru." In Vrndavana the jata-guru, caste gosvami, they do like that. He'll not touch his water even, and still, he is disciple. He'll not take his food, he'll not touch his water, and still, he's guru.

That's all. In Vrndavana it is going on, large... So many visitors come. They are victimized. Cheating is going on. You have to be careful. Otherwise very risky. Vipralipsa. One of the qualification of conditioned souls is to cheat others and be cheated. Vanchita vanchaka. (Conversation: Bogus Gurus — April 25, 1977, Bombay)

However, if one simply imitates advanced spiritual life, he will fall down, just like the sahajiyas in Vrndavana. (Caitanya Caritamrta; Madhya 11.176 Purport)

That is my Guru Maharaja's gift. He first of all started that there is no need of going to Vrndavana and imitate the Gosvamis. Live in big, big cities, in big, big palatial houses, but preach Krsna consciousness. (Lecture from Srila Prabhupada: Srimad-Bhagavatam 7th Canto — Calcutta, March 7, 1972)

ALL THAT YOU EAT

You stated was that residents of Vrndavana have no need to offer food to Krsna. It is all considered offered. Srila Prabhupada orders everyone to offer every bit of food to Krsna and then you state it is not required.

"Therefore if we promise that we shall not eat anything which is not offered to Krsna, that is tapasya. If you don't go to the restaurant and eat anything nonsense, that is pravrtti. But if you want to stop that restaurant-going, then you take Krsna prasadam; krsna bora daya moy kori bare jihva joy sva-prasada-anna dilo bhai. Krsna is ready, so many nice, palatable dishes; you take and stop this restaurant-going. This is Krsna's mercy. Patram puspam phalam toyam yo me bhaktya prayacchati. Krsna does not say "Bring something from the restaurant" or this or that. He says, patram puspam phalam toyam yo me bhaktya prayacchati: anything, little leaf, little flower, little water. Krsna is not hungry, but Krsna is so kind that He has come to you, so that you can touch Him, you can dress Him, you can decorate Him, you can offer Him, you can live with Him as servant, as friend, as son, as lover. In so many ways, Krsna is giving you chance. (His Divine Grace Srila Bhaktisiddhanta Sarasvati Gosvami Prabhupada's Disappearance Day, Lecture — Bombay, December 22, 1975)

There are so many times Srila Prabhupada told his disciples to offer all their food to Krsna.

OTHER PUBLICATIONS FROM RVC

FORTUNATE SOULS – THE BHAKTA PROGRAM MANUAL: by HH Danavir Goswami. The popular, standard guide to recruiting and training new devotees in ISKCON. Congregation devotees also use it. (760 pages, hardcover, stitch binding, 64 pages of illustrations including dozens of original drawings) ($40)

"It is a masterpiece." – Indradyumna Swami

"*Fortunate Souls* provides an important spiritual road map helping devotees to assist others on the journey back to Godhead."
– Professor E. Burke Rochford; Middlebury College

THIS IS GOD? (Vaisnava Society Journal #1): By HH Danavir Goswami and other ISKCON writers. 70 pages, 8.5 x 11 inches, color covers, excellent graphics, includes an amazing article of Vedic evidence predicting Lord Caitanya; the size of the universe; the author of the Vedas, etc. ($4)

DIKSA DIKSA: By leading ISKCON devotees. Thoroughly analyzes and discredits the modern "Ritvic Theory" using scripture, logic, evidence and history. 120 pages, coilbound. ($5)

THE LEGACY GOES ON (Vaisnava Society Journal #2): By HH Danavir Goswami and other ISKCON writers. Includes an interesting article debunking anti-dairy beliefs; plus a special look at Visnujana Swami, an all-ladies temple, etc. 60 pages, 8.5. x 11 inches. ($4)

HIS DIVINE GRACE: Danavir Goswami tells of his unique experiences with Srila Prabhupada from 1970 to 1977. Includes episodes from Los Angeles, San Francisco, Berkeley, Portland, Chicago, London, Mayapur and Vrndavana. Hardbound, 240 pages includes 24 color pages of photographs. ($15)

"*His Divine Grace* is a treasure."
–Kumsi Krishna (retired engineer)

"Fascinating account of life within the movement."
–Dru Sefton (Feature writer for Kansas City Star)

VEDIC PARADIGM: A marvelous panoramic survey of Vedic knowledge and culture systematically discussing topics from Vedic morality to mystic powers. Designed for college-level students by Danavir Goswami using writings from Srila Prabhupada and his disciples. Hardbound, 384 pages. ($20)

"*Vedic Paradigm* should be distributed widely and given to every college student in the land."
– Wallace Dorian (freelance writer)

POISON ANTIDOTE: More than a dozen astute ISKCON writers exhaustively repudiate a modern conjecture that Srila Prabhupada was poisoned by his disciples. 114 pages, coilbound. ($5)

THE KRISHNA ERA 5227 (Vaisnava Society Journal #3): Primarily written by HH Danavir Goswami. A compilation of essays discussing reinitiation, sports, kirtana, the exact date of Lord Krisna's appearance, etc. 128 pages, coilbound. ($5)

RUPANUGA VEDIC COLLEGE PROSPECTUS: A complete and fascinating description of ISKCON's first Vedic Seminary College. Includes course outlines, degree programs, bhakti sastri and shakti vaibhava programs, application forms, student handbook, etc. 160 pages, softbound. ($2)

CHANGE OF HEART/ THE AGE OF KALI (125 pages; softbound) By His Holiness Danavir Goswami and His Grace Yamunacarya dasa. Contains two plays written for and performed by KrishnaFest Theatre Company across the US. Change of Heart tells of a young man's attempts to become a devotee of Krishna. The Age of Kali depicts the evil influence of the age we live in and how it can be counteracted. ($5)

POCKET TEMPLE SONG BOOK (58 pages; soft) For new devotees in the temple and in the congregation. Contains all the songs sung in ISKCON temple programs. Ideally fits in the pocket. Designed and used by the Bhakta Program Institute and Rupanuga Vedic College. ($2)

UTTAMA SLOKA (310 pages; hardcover and coilbound;) An extensive array of verses quoted by Srila Prabhupada. Includes the entire Vaisnava Song Book, Brahma Samhita, etc. Compiled and edited by His Holiness Danavir Goswami. ($20)

RAH TAH TAH HARE KRISHNA (Vaisnava Society Journal Vol. 4) (125 pages; softbound) Includes articles by ISKCON devotees on chanting the holy names, Vedic etiquette, asramas, academic studies in Vaisnavism, personal closeups, contemporary issues, and book distribution. ($5)

ISKCON IN THE MIDDLE EAST (Vaisnava Society Journal Vol. 4) 125 pages softbound; Includes articles by ISKCON devotees on remembering Tribhuvannatha Prabhu, the Druze leaders visit ISKCON India, Guru in the Morning, brahmacarya, infallible Srila Prabhupada, pramanam—Vedic or experimental evidence, the Karmic Trust Fund, etc. ($5)

Audio CDs & Cassettes:

LOVE OF KRISHNA by Premadhana: Premadhan, led by HH Danavir Goswami (lead singer), combines Vedic and Western instrumentation to accompany the maha mantra and other traditional Vaisnava bhajanas and kirtanas. 60 minutes, stereo, studio recording.CD: $15,
Cassette: $8

THE MAGIC IS THE CHANTING by KrishnaFest Band: A classic live-studio album recorded in San Diego during KrishnaFest Band's heyday. Album features HH Danavir Goswami, HG Mahatma Prabhu and HH Gunagrahi Goswami among others. East-west blend of several Hare Krishna mantra renditions. 60 minutes, stereo. CD: $15, Cassette: $8

VAISNAVA BHAJANAS by HH Danavir Goswami. Traditional ISKCON bhajanas accompanied with tamboura, mrdanga, karatalas and harmonium. 60 minutes, stereo, studio recording.
CD: $15, Cassette: $8

Video Cassette:

THE AGE OF KALI by KrishnaFest Theatre Company. A live performance of the newest version of this ISKCON classic. Filmed in Alachua, Florida. Features: Yamunacarya dasa, Radha-vinode dasa, Danavir Goswami, Candrasekhara dasa, Dhirodatta dasa, Paul Suhor and others. 45 minutes; ($20)